DATE DUE

MAY 0-1 1996			
GAYLORD			PRINTED IN U.S.A.

Duraflex

Manifestations of Thought

by
Molana-al-Moazam
Hazrat Shah Maghsoud Sadegh Angha
"Pir Oveyssi"

Sadig'Anga

School of Islamic Sufism ®
Maktab Tarighe Oveyssi Shahmaghsoudi

Shahmaghsoudi (Angha) Heritage Series on Sufism

UNIVERSITY
PRESS OF
AMERICA

Lanham • New York • London

Copyright © 1988 by

the School of Islamic Sufism

University Press of America,® Inc.

4720 Boston Way
Lanham, MD 20706

3 Henrietta Street
London WC2E 8LU England

Library of Congress Cataloging-in-Publication Data

Angha, Sadegh, 1916–
[Ma' ālim al-fikr. English]
Manifestations of thought / by Maghsoud Sadegh Angha.
p. cm.—(Shahmaghsoudi (Angha) heritage series on Sufism)
Translation of: Ma' ālim al-fikr.
1. Sufism—Miscellanea. I. Title. II. Sereis: Sādiq 'Anqā,
1916–Shahmaghsoudi (Angha) heritage series on Sufism.
BP189.23.S2313   1988
297'.4—dc 19   88–20599 CIP
ISBN 0–8191–7135–2 (alk. paper)
ISBN 0–8191–7136–0 (pbk. : alk. paper)

All University Press of America books are produced on acid-free paper.
The paper used in this publication meets the minimum requirements of
American National Standard for Information Sciences—Permanence of Paper
for Printed Library Materials, ANSI Z39.48–1984.

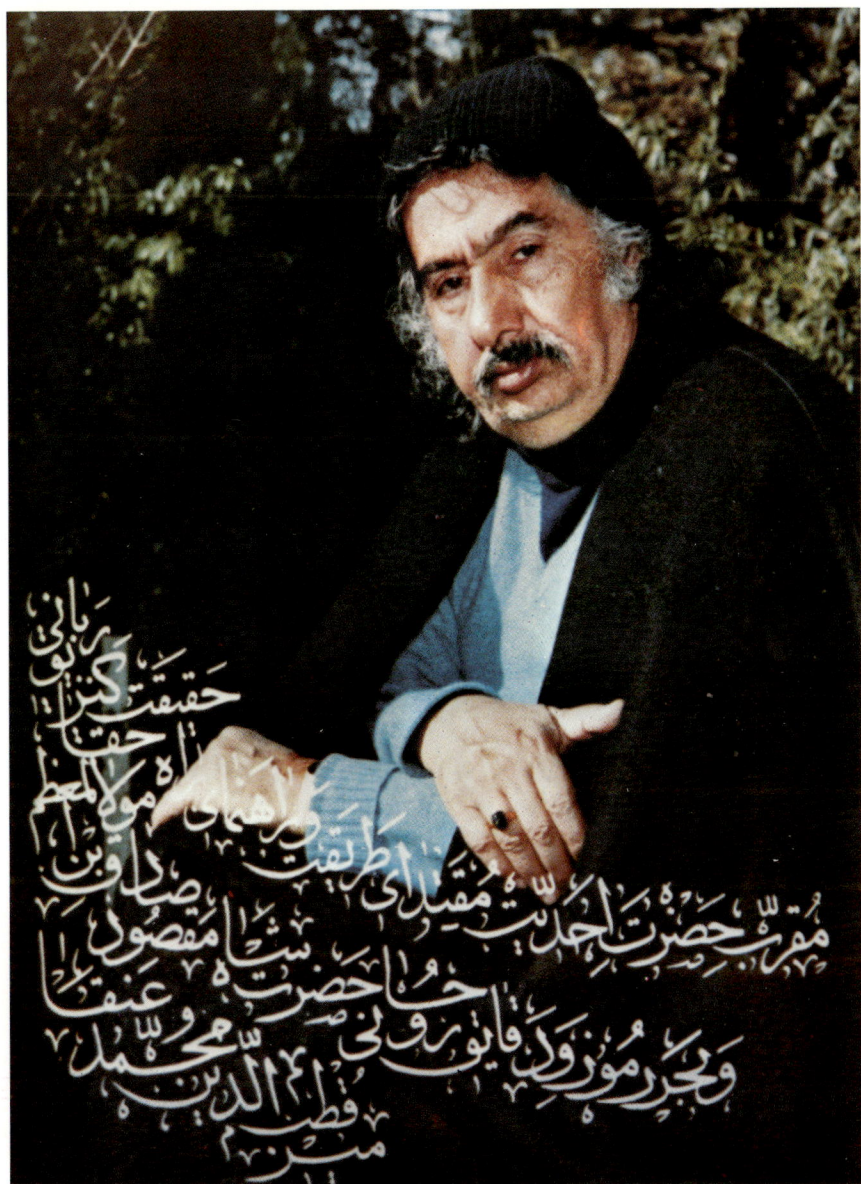

Molana-al-Moazam Hazrat Shah Maghsoud Sadegh Angha
"Pir Oveyssi"

CONTENTS

Publisher's Note

Foreword... i

Preface vii

Introduction....................................... 1

*If only the alphabet of the one
spiritual book were revealed
to man, and the secret
of the book of the soul*

*discovered, he would need none
of the words sealed
in silent books, and yet
would know the story whole.*

First Manifesto 9

*The true scientists generally consider
The past science merely as an introductory chapter;
And reckon that the truly new spur
Of knowledge springs from one's own true nature.
The fountainhead of the knowledge's spring
Is none but one's own essence, one's inner being.*

Second Manifesto 21

*Existence is the subject of a mysterious fate —
In a riddle-like fashion — apparently without meaning!
An individual entity; be it a speck of dust,
Or a human being — seems to have little free will in it!*

*In reality, everything is utterly dependent on, and a microstate
of, a Universal Grand Existence, a Supreme Being,
Encompassing the boundless universe; each particle is an entity just
Limited completely if seen through the rather limited slit*

*Of the lens of man; but the Gate
Of Existence offers a view quite unlimited, all-compassing!
And so each individual entity is — as it must
Be — free, being a parcel of the free totality, sans limit.*

Third Manifesto 35

A true and noble society is keenly responsible
To promote sciences and other fields of learning,
And to encourage scientists and others with a yearning
For the pursuit of knowledge.

Fourth Manifesto 45

If we shan't straighten and rectify
our outer appearance
and our inner selves,
the picture of our past days
will be most frightening, and painful instance
of existence, an unbearable and shameful far cry!

Fifth Manifesto 61

Particles, like numbers, apparently seem discrete,
Confined in space, finite quantities, pretty petty entities.
In reality, however, if we meet
Their latent, potential form and feat,
We realize they extend unbound, limitlessly touching the infinities.

But in this world, we can find nothing that defies regulation
— Either in form or in substance, in meaning or in appearance —
That acts in dire contradiction
To the laws of Existence, under random fiction.
The rational element is ever present, in every turn and nuance!

So, particles within limited bound are finite; only elemental
Forms, with a negligible role as to the properties of the whole,
Or the absolute, or the monumental.
But they also possess a transcendental
Norm, where they're one with the universe, the infinite Soul.

Sixth Manifesto 71

The greater man's awakening
The greater his knowledge of Existence;
The greater opening of his inner eyes and vision,
The more acute his own awareness of his being
Full of ignorance — to gain knowledge's essence,
The above is the wise's first step, the firmest decision!

Seventh Manifesto 85

Death is an evolutionary step, indeed,
Toward lifting the dark veils drawn upon
The infinite absolute!
But life and death serve the same creed —
This paramount truth upon us must dawn.
For, who can refute
That life and death are reflections that feed
The vision from the mirror of the universal pantheon,
The Existence's stages by statute!

Eighth Manifesto.................................... 103

Man's natural, unquenchable
Endless expection,
Desires and longing
Are all layers and linings
Of thick veils of mummification
Over his eyes, making him unable
To see the truth, covering and killing
His own inner vision;
And that's the reason
Why man, like the victim of treason,
Has remained away from his paragon
Happiness, acting like the blind, taking the fake for the real.

Genealogy of Maktab Tarighe Oveyssi Shahmaghsoudi .. 117

Partial List of Works by the Author 119

Glossary of Selected Names 121

This verse rendition of the original Persian prose of the *Manifestations of Thought* by Molana-al-Moazam Hazrat Shah Maghsoud Sadegh Angha, Pir Tarighe Oveyssi Shahmaghsoudi has evolved from the collaboration of Ms. Avideh Shashaani and Mr. Ashok Sinha. Ms. Shashaani's training in the discipline of *Erfan* (Sufism)—as the way to the cognition of the realities beyond the scope of the senses and the intellect—and Mr. Sinha's training as a physicist paved the groundwork for an indepth study and interpretive English translation of *Manifestations of Thought*. This cooperation itself is symbolic of what the book portrays, the interrelationship of physics and metaphysics in presenting every form of life on the canvas of Existence—the message that bridges the separation between religion and science, and answers the penetrating questions of the philosopher and the scientist alike about the reality of life, and the roles of the physical and metaphysical forces in moulding and determining man's steps on the chart of Existence.

It should be emphasized that the present volume may be characterized as more of a trans-creation inspired by the original Persian prose book than a pure translation. Thus the transformation represented herein includes not only linguistic—Persian to English—but also prose to poetry and, to a considerable degree, a free paraphrasing of the original text.

Ms. Shashaani, a native Iranian, educated in the U.S. from childhood, holds degrees in Psychology, Educational Planning and Management, and Islamic Sufism and Philosophy. She has had extensive experience in the field of rehabilitation counseling, disability prevention, and program design and implementation working with Third World governments as well as the

United Nations and its Agencies. Since her engagement with Maktab Tarighe Oveyssi Shahmaghsoudi (School of Islamic Sufism), she has integrated her educational and professional experiences, guided by the discipline of *Erfan*, to teach classes on prevention of stress related disorders, meditation, and Practical Sufism.

Mr. Ashok K. Sinha was born in a village (Kadma) of Hazaribagh, in the Bihar State of India on 8 January 1943. He completed his education in Patna (India) and the United States, earning M.Sc. and Ph.D degrees in Physics in 1965 and 1971, respectively. Presently he works as a member of Technical Staff of the International Telecommunications Satellite Organization (INTELSAT) in Washington, D.C., in the field of satellite communications.

In the area of Physics, Mr. Sinha's especial interests include particle physics and astrophysics, which relate to the fundamental structure and origin of matter and the universe at large. As a Research Fellow of NASA and subsequently while working with COMSAT and INTELSAT, he has made a number of contributions on atmospheric and ionospheric modeling, systems modeling and optimization of satellite communications systems, inter-satellite links, optical communication, which have been, published in various professional journals or presented in international conferences in which he represented INTELSAT. One of his papers introduced the concept of an integrated global network configuration of communications satellites, and was awarded the Piero Fanti International Prize in 1982.

Better understanding of the deeper realities of nature, as well as of the human mind and heart, has been the source of inspiration behind his pursuit of literature, religion, and philosophy in addition to physics. He is an ardent admirer of Sufi philosophy and poetry. Literature, especially poetry, has been a keen interest of his. He writes poetry in his native tongue, Hindi, as well as in English, and has completed verse translations of the well known classic Sanskrit scripture of India—the Gita; Omar

Khayam's Rubayat, and some of the works of the famed Lebanese poet, Kahlil Gibran into Hindi. These and collections of his poems in Hindi and English are planned to be published shortly.

Manifestations of Thought marks the commencement of UPA's publication of the *Shahmaghsoudi (Angha) Heritage Series on Sufism.*

"What exists, in *absolute rapture*, glorifies the *essence of being.*"

Calligraphy by the hand of Molana-al-Moazam Hazrat Shah Maghsoud Sadegh Angha

*"In The Name Of The Almighty One
Everpresent—The Eternal One"*

Whatever the universe portrays,
Is but a reflection of My Face.

"What is the particle?", they ask.
  Say, *"The sun!"*

"What is the water drop?", they ask.
  Say, *"The ocean!"*

Behold the wine and the cup, to see
The wine as the Essence, and its attributes,
  The world in its entirety.

Of the union of the wine and the cup you ask.
From purity divine, the cup knows naught
  But the Wine.

Ghazaliat
by
Molana-al-Moazam Hazrat Shah Maghsoud Sadegh Angha
"Pir Oveyssi"

***

i

The quintessence of love and knowledge, Molana-al-Moazam Hazrat Shah Maghsoud Sadegh Angha, the forty-first Great *Pir* (Spiritual Teacher) of Maktab Tarighe Oveyssi (School of Islamic Sufism) graced the earth with his presence on the fourth of February, 1916 in Tehran, Iran. The foundations for his teachings and the lineage of his School are traced directly through forty eminent Masters to Molana Hazrat Oveys Gharani, whose method for divine revelations and cognition of truth was confirmed by the Holy Prophet of Islam, Hazrat Rassoul Akram Mohammad Mostafa (peace and blessings upon him). The Cloak of the Prophet which had been passed on from the Holy Prophet Abraham, was bestowed upon Molana Hazrat Oveys Gharani, by his holiness fourteen centuries ago. The Holy Cloak, symbolic of the divine knowledge transmitted to man by God, has found its eloquent and inspiring voice in the personage of the forty-two eminent and illustrious Masters of Maktab Tarighe Oveyssi Shahmaghsoudi throughout the centuries to the present time.

Erfan, equated with Sufism in the West, in its absolute sense means "Self-Knowledge". The *Aref* (Sufi) is he who has attained the highest state of "Self-Knowledge" through annihilation in God.

The message of *Erfan* is a precise and serious message, intended for those who are genuinely interested in undertaking a research into their own "self" to discover the cause for their being, the meaning of life, and ultimately, their course beyond death. The central teaching of *Erfan* is: Each being has within itself all knowledge of its being, its course in presenting itself as a being and knowledge of where it will go. In other words, each being is a complete book that can only be read by the being itself.

What is the way to attain this knowledge?

Erfan encompasses both the physical and the metaphysical sciences. During each age this knowledge has been taught by the one and rightful *Pir* (Spiritual Master) of the School to its students. "Knowing" in the absolute sense, innate and inward cognition, and an unquenchable love for knowledge and learning are the bases of instruction. In the School of Islamic Sufism, the constant, unchangeable law is "Oneness"; physics and metaphysics are of one entity and follow this law. Nature, in the eyes of the beholder, is many faceted and ever changing: Metaphysic's penetration of the universe is so precise that what appears variable is but a manifestation of the One Absolute Knowledge, unchangeable and eternal.

Erfan is the religion of Existence. Religion is not confined by boundaries and limitations; it transcends manmade adversitites and the prejudices of societies and cultures. Religion means *stability in reality*, attained by the serious and dedicated student of *Erfan* through his own experience in his innermost being. The essential goal and message of all the Prophets is based on the unchangeable law of "Self-Knowledge."

Molana Hazrat Salaheddin Ali Nader Shah Angha writes in *The Wealth of Solouk*: "The *Aref* believes in the Oneness of Existence. In His innermost book is unlimited Existence; there is no other but He, and He is Absolute. Thus, all possibilities and qualities, all attributes and states, and all conditions that are manifested before man are bestowed by His boundless grace and His Essence. This is not in the sense of separation or duality between Him and man, but of the Oneness of Existence incarnate in man in the full horizon of his awareness. He is not in things. He is unquantifiable. Appearances are the reflections of Truth, and Truth is the source of all manifestations. He is the essence of goodness and beauty, the summit of perfection and grace. 'Self' is a token of His blessings, and 'soul', the breath of His ever penetrating love. What exists cannot be other than it is, and absolute cognition for man is beholding the Absolute Truth through the journey of 'Self' to 'I'."

Molana-al-Moazam Hazrat Shah Maghsoud Sadegh Angha, known to his students in the West as Professor Angha, studied the discipline of *Erfan* (Sufism) for over thirty years under the guidance of his father Molana-al-Moazam Hazrat Mir Ghotbeddin Mohammad Angha, the fortieth eminent Master of the School. His in-depth knowledge of the sciences, law, philosophy, literature, arts, and religion encapsulates the timeless knowledge of the *Aref* into words that are in harmony with the inquisitive mind of the scientist, the imagination of the poet, the logic of the philosopher, and the aspirant heart of the mystic.

Professor Angha's mastery of the sciences and his great facility in applying the principles of *Erfan* to respond to the most vital questions facing contemporary man have gained him respect and admiration by scholars and scientists throughout the world.

Professor Angha's words are those of divine revelation and inspiration—declaring the laws of Existence—the awakening call of Existence that sets into motion the inner core of the listener. Professor Angha has written over 150 books in poetry and prose, crossing and integrating the boundaries of physics and metaphysics—astrophysics, particle physics, quantum electrodynamics, biophysics, cell physiology, evolution, genetics, psychophysiology, human magnetics, aging, cancer, death, healing, consciousness, telepathy, astral body projection, clairvoyance, monism, existence, cognition—under the orchestration of one absolute law: "La-elaha-ella-Allah"—resonating the Oneness of Existence.

Molana Salaheddin Ali Nader Shah ibn Molana-al-Moazam Hazrat Shah Maghsoud Sadegh Angha, who succeeded his father as the forty second eminent *Pir* of this sacred School of "Self-Knowledge" with over 300,000 students worldwide, states in the introduction to *Al-Rasa'el*:

> Knowledge of the truth of man and existence has a course which goes beyond the basic preliminary messages and discoveries, and ends with absolute cognition. This innate

drive and curiosity has determined man's destiny and fate and has completed the pages of self-knowledge with the humming love-call of its seekers throughout the centuries; and in each age, according to the will of Existence, a new branch appears on the tree of Life - the preemptor - to guide and save the sons of man. Existence created the beautiful in manifestations, and beauty has been veiled in meaning; and the *Aref* is the unveiled beauty.

Erfan is the science of Existence and the living heritage of man. The *Aref*, the symbol of the most exalted state of man, is the clear mirror of Existence. His words awaken man to his noble but forgotten "Self"—the motion toward a constant state of freedom and tranquility. His mission is to teach man to unearth, develop, and unite his powers in the discovery of the laws of existence implanted within his own being, and his intricate and unified relationship with the infinite universe.

The message of *Erfan* is crystal clear. Molana Salaheddin Ali Nader Shah ibn Molana-al-Moazam Hazrat Shah Maghsoud Sadegh Angha, the *Aref* of our time, has stated in his teachings: "You have all the knowledge you need; ask Existence, God, Allah, Jehovah, Christ, Buddha, Brahma, whomever or whatever you consider as the source and pillar of your existence—but ask in earnest with sincerity, honesty and love—to show you the way to your true being, so that you may embark on your journey of Self-Knowledge with certainty, without doubt. God's message for man throughout time has been: *Grow before winter comes.*"

Lynn E. Wilcox, Ph.D.
California State University, Sacramento
February 4, 1988

A bird takes to wings
And soars up in the sky;
A bee hums and sings,
And the flowers offer sundry

Gifts for honey's harvest.
A baby's born in the world:
What treasures in his chest
Lie undiscovered, unfathomed!

Does he ever contemplate. . . .
What the body's relative roles
Are? How actions act; the fate
Formulates? Who harks the soul's

Clarion call, the Nature's voice?
And in Existence's edifice,
God's glimpses gains, to rejoice?
In each particle, the Absolute sees? . . .

Such queries, quizzes, quest
Are far from new! From the very young
Moments of the race, the noblest
Of men, as Hazrat Molana Shah Maghsoud Sadegh Angha

Has done, have endeavoured
And discovered answers to these eternal
Questions, belabored and favored
Discovering the Truth, Knowledge's kernel,

To any other reward the earth
And life could offer. The wise,
Recognizing the bondage of birth,
Strive to regain the lost paradise.

In this saga of the sages,
"Manifestations of Thought",
By Hazrat Molana Angha, says
What a true seeker must've sought.

***

"Manifestations of Thought" bears
Such a unique, enlightening synthesis
Between religion and science, that seers
Alone are capable of capturing like this.

The mystery of the nature's work,
And the universe's continual unfolding,
The questions that perpetually lurk
In man's mind, in search of meaning

Behind the Existence, and transformations
Of the cosmos and the consciousness —
Are dealt here, with apt illustrations,
And due clarity, and forthright stress.

Physics and other branches of science
Are generally regarded as disjoint
From religion, philosophy, metaphysics, chance -
Encounter of the human faculty with the point -

Location in space-time where reason
Is no obstacle to spiritual inspiration
Or covets supremacy, or commits treason;
Where scientific pursuit is one with self-realization.

"Manifestations of Thought" so beautifully blends
Sharp observations of Electrodynamics with deep reflections
On the spiritual identity of man, that it surely lends
A helping hand to the greater meaning of actions

And reactions, waves and particles, planets
And stars, birth and evolution of the universe.
With great precision it expounds familiar scientific facets
And then lets them expand with interest, to reimburse

Tributes to universal truths rediscovered
Pertaining to the human nature, social trends,
The nature's ways, and Existence's will, unheard
Of—it's a treasure whose credit never ends!

***

The content of this precious treatise
Dwells on the relationship of the soul and God,
Of the self and the Existence, that lies
At the core of man's ultimate vision broad.

The contemplation of the grand scheme
Of Existence: of man and his soul,
Of the Nature and the universe, of the Godhead supreme
Is the Sufi's chosen path; the cherished goal

Being the rediscovery of the "I" that within each
Of us lies dormant, awaiting the awakening!
This path to unravel and expound and teach
Is the mission of Shahmaghsoudi School—the Knowledge
    Spring!

This tradition has continued ov'r many generations.
Thus the torch was passed from the Forty-First
Master: Molana Hazrat Shah Maghsoud—our venerations
To him—to the Forty-Second teacher: his son, well versed

In the highest order of sublime spiritual knowledge,
Enlightened Hazrat Salaheddin Ali Nader Shah Angha.
I reverently bow to pay my tribute to their vital knowledge
And spirit leading the pupils, the Almighty willing!

The great inspiration and whatever little ability
That came to serve in the materialization
Of the present work surely benefit from their felicity:
Their unseen hand was indeed behind the translation

Not only from conception to creation, thought to word,
But their benediction transpires Persian into English.
It is not just out of courtesy that they're admired:
Their gift's stamp is all-over—from the start to finish.

Eight Manifestos the present volume comprises,
Each dealing in a lucidly treated theme;
The readers' hearts are illumined by the ray-like sentences,
And throughout the pearls of truth marvellously gleam.

The First Manifesto discusses how discoveries are made;
The Second deals with the question of human free will;
The Third presents a discourse of how society comes to aid
Science's cause, becoming the beneficiary of its lofty will.

The other Manifestos bestow similar enlightening touches
On subjects ranging from the earth to the heavens.
A wholesome integration is evident in areas as much as
One can conceive: from particle to the very Existence!

***

Written originally in fine Persian,
This work, set in simple terms, modern
Contexts, excels as an exposition
Of Sufism, for those who yearn

To expand the grand vistas of ways
Of life, schools of thought, realization
Of the sublime truth. The superb essays —
Leading the spirit through the mind's sublimation —

Of the original have been put
In a verse form in this translation,
With a lot of liberty, with due salute;
The message being my main motivation!

It's been a great honor, a true
Privilege to have had this
Excellent opportunity to cast into
English this spiritual treatise—nay, bliss!

For me, this undertaking would've been
Literally impossible—not just hard —
But for Ms. Avideh Shashaani's keen
Assistance and exchanges. A reward

This experience of rewording
The great venerated Master's message
Noble, through the nimble meaning
Interpreted by his able student to me, page

By page, phase by phase, has
Indeed been—not enough
Thanks can be given for this! As
The soul immortal changes the body stuff

Through the alternate passages
Of life after life, through the maze;
So also, the truth of great messages
Can be manifested in many formats, languages!

With my total ignorance of Persian (in
Addition to a great many fine things),
She alone must this effort's credit win,
I alone claim blame for its shortcomings.

***

So, finally, the question returns
To the original point that vies
With the birds and the bees! The human earns
"Manifestations of Thought", to rise!

I genuinely hope, as the author
Did, that the readers truly benefit
From these lines, giving to our labor
Its true reward, and grand success to it.

Ashok K. Sinha
Washington, DC (USA)
10 May, 1987

پدیده های فکر

Manifestations of Thought

بُوالعَلَى اللّٰهُ

"In God's Great Name"

If only the alphabet of the one
spiritual book were revealed
to man, and the secret
of the book of the soul

discovered, he would need none
of the words sealed
in silent books, and yet
would know the story whole.

From the writings of
Molana Hazrat Mir Ghotbeddin Mohammad Angha
"Pir Oveyssi"

***

To guide the reader to the truth sublime,
  To awaken his self-awareness in its search —
I intend not, by any means, but at this time,
  My solemn mission is to pass on the torch

1

Of my own awakening, to simply convey
   The truth as I discovered it, in pieces and bits,
And continue to do so, each passing day,
   Throughout my life, through its crests and its pits.

***

But if you were to ask—why I wish so
   To offer these revelations of mine to you;
This I would have to say—Do the sound waves go
   In search of receivers to be received? No, they do

Not; the waves simply emanate from the source
   And are naturally and precisely received by the receivers
That happen to be there, in their course,
   And in keeping with their capacities. So also the readers

And recipients of various orders and inclinations
   Will automatically, involuntarily, and inevitably receive
Whatever truth any source, with exhilarations
   Or with solemnity, does emit—per the levels they achieve.

***

And the fruits of such occurrences do not just perish!
   Well, little does occur here without reason or rhyme.
The path of truth wins Man's lasting cherish,
   And it leads one to triumph, without limit, beyond time.

***

The expositions contained within these pages reflect
   My inner revelations, born out of my living
Existence, in full harmony with my Self, and my direct
   Experiences. For, while I am not the wisest being

Among men of my time, and my word
   Is not ordained to assume the coveteous place

Of the unyielding Laws of Nature; it's to be heard
   Not in vain, nor to fill the reader's mind, and face,

With trifles, and superficial wonders, to be of no significance
   Or authenticity that the inner revelation brings;
For, the pride in borrowed word and copied stance
   Is hindrance to true knowledge—from it no truth ever
   springs.

***

With a little attention, one knows that no word
   — However logical and beautiful—can ever convey
The real essence, the paramount truth: if only heard
   Through the ears and mind that the listener may

Employ for the purpose—something more is required.
   By uttering the word - "water", for instance, one never
Conjures up the same flavor, the true experience, as a tired,
   Thirst-stricken man derives from drinking real water.

Words at best construe transient shadows, and fleeting images,
   Barely bearing a generic analogue to the reality —
That the mind might only reminisce, or have forgotten for ages;
   Even the weightiest of words lack the genuine quality.

Thus exchange of thoughts wearing a wordy cloak and form
   Is an exercise in futility—as one readily observes,
Especially when the speaker (as is commonly a norm),
   Himself knows not the story his word proverbs.

In other words, words do not necessarily bear
   The finest similarity to the meaning they espouse.
Furthermore, to add to the problem, listeners, as they hear,
   Make projection of their meanings, simply because

They must interpret them based on their very own
   Past experiences and collective sensibility built thereupon.

And since it's different sets of experiences we've known,
　　We each conceive differently, having a different constitution.

So, true exchange between two people can only take place
　　On the basis of commonality of mentality and experience;
This, then, is the delicate premise that one must face
　　In building understanding between true friends; and, hence,

In absence of such a basis, one remains just a stranger,
　　Knowing not what transpires, though the words may fly by.
The speaker and the listener would then converse no better
　　Than those speaking different languages, however they may
　　try.

***

Descartes, in "Discourse on Method", has the saying:
　　"No one learns as much from another as from his own
Personal urges and creative yearning for learning."
　　How often one finds that, after a discourse controversy-
　　prone,

One thinks that the specific points have been fully grasped —
　　Every word of the speaker truly comprehended;
But, on query, the listener is found to somehow have adapted
　　Quite a different meaning; with a deviant picture to have
　　ended.

As words are simply symbolic abstract representations
　　Of objects and attributes that are conventionally shared,
And, as such, are used for common communications
　　Among people; they fail their mission if they're aired

For expressing the sublime and intimate meanings, the
　　innermost
　　Truths transcendental—for how can they bind

4

In characters divinity supreme, in paper-cups the airy winter
  frost?
  If one contrived to do so, one'll naturally find

That the conclusions turn negative, and confusing gets the goal.
  Thus, a reliance on mere words for the expression and
    communication
Of the truth innermost and of the evolution of the soul
  Will only lead to the gaol of words, and shackles of
    recollection.

For, Leibniz did say - "When the quality of an object
  Is in harmony with its appearance, then only it's possible
To offer a true description, and a definition fully straight;
  Otherwise it's merely a name, an artifice artificial,

Uncertain in its scope, and inaccurate, and inadequate —
  Just a word, that may be even misleading full-fledgedly;
Referring to opposite attributes and, at any rate,
  Rendering expositions incomplete, and misfiring single-
    handedly."

                           ***

My purpose above is not to undermine the agreement
  Among people in the society about the usage of the word;
But to point out the truth that the Truth can be present,
  But may not be illuminated, or understood, or heard

By words' power alone—the power of the spirit,
  The aptitude of the soul and a complete mental elevation
To embody consonance with the deep meanings implicit
  Are needed for us to know the Truth; through sublimation

Of our senses and sensibility and of the mind into a pure
  Experience of the soul, can only we know the Truth;

And once the Truth does find inner cognition, it's sure,
No word can obscure it—through illness, mutilation, or
death.

***

If it's accepted that the tidiness and purity of its pages,
And clarity of a book on the shelf, and its general look
Are indispensable for the comprehension of what it says;
Then the indispensability of the study of the venerated book

Of the Self is self-evident—as it is the faithful mirror
Of the world in existence. Thus I would certainly recommend
That instead of investing much time in outer
Silent books, one should definitely try to spend

Every effort to study truly the book of oneself,
One's inherent personality and one's innermost identity; so,
the
Spiritual awakening and knowledge can help
Bridge the gap between the heart and that entity

We commonly call the brain, so that it can also receive
Readily the waves of true and precise meanings
From the sources radiating those, ready to give —
The thinkers and creators who, amidst paucity of the soul,
are kings.

***

As the truth can't be captured in debates and reasoning,
It is urged that the readers of this treatise;
Instead of analyzing it outwardly, churning out critiques
stunning,
Examine and test, extend and complement its contents, and
revise.

6

My great Master—my father—with his great mentorship,
  And with patience and wisdom, and inner spiritual teaching,
Guided my mind in the right direction, with care and apt
    leadership,
  Preventing it from deviations; lest I should fall, not reaching

The peak of learning he offered without selfishness or ambition;
  And all I've to offer is but what I learnt from him.
With this gift—through my writing, work and contemplation,
  If I'm able to lighten and brighten a single candle dim

To take a single small step in the direction of the good
  Of the great human family—I will not have spent
My life in vain; and if not, I'd have done little that I should
  Have; uplifting no soul, mine will be far from content.

Sadegh Angha
February 1954
Tehran

The true scientists generally consider
The past science merely as an introductory chapter;
And reckon that the truly new spur
Of knowledge springs from one's own true nature.
The fountainhead of the knowledge's spring
Is none but one's own essence, one's inner being.

***

What scientists miraculously unearth through time
  Is barely a trifle introductory page
To the book of supreme knowledge, the truth sublime,
  For the seeker venturing his inner self to envisage —

As the foundation of all absolute knowledge,
  As the prolific pillar that perpetually lends
Support and credence, and timeless tutelage,
  To the spirit, in its quest of the most enlightening trends.

For, if we were to consider the fertile minds
  Of scientists as the symbol of the grand sum-total
Of human knowledge, of the ultimate realities of all kinds,
  Then, the loftiest summit, the last hypothetical

Vestige, the farthest imaginable aim or destination
  Would have, no doubt, been reached by this time;
But, nay! The fountainhead of the faculty, the very foundation
  Of the facility scientists possess, resides in the prime

Of their being, in their true consciousness, their inner selves;
  And, so, they themselves regard an omni-scient and omni-
    present

Absolute Self—that simultaneously dwells
　　From here to the infinity, from now to the eternity, the
　　　　inherent

Source of their inspiration; a strong, stable, boundless focus;
　　The perennial, unswerving basis of their true personality.
And they can go a full circle, all around, in a locus,
　　Led to the higher planes, guided by this singular centrality,

Starting from the true, yet an infinitesimal
　　Point of spiritual concentration; and thus at any turn
And point, they make their excursion, their perpetual
　　Evolutionary journeys, their existence multiplying knowledge
　　　　as a churn.

Although they can never quite reach the end,
　　They receive the bliss and the benefit of their being
At any point of their existence; and never tend
　　To get confused by the extraneous limit of their being.

It is the spiritual attainment that frees the soul
　　Of the scientist; so he does not get bound or constrained
By the periphery of any hypothesis, any discovery, or pole
　　Of thought, nor considers it the supreme goal gained;

But, rather, whatever ground he gains, or root uncovers,
　　Through his studies—he regards a gift, filling the empty
　　　　wares
Of his thoughts, treating them as blessed ushers,
　　For introduction to his real quest in life's thoroughfares.

If we view the horizons unveiled by Astronomy,
　　For instance, through its observations on the stars and
　　　　planets,
It would seem they feature diverse forms of energy:
　　(e.g., Electromagnetic, atomic, solar radiation, particle jets.)

Thus, the problems and solutions of darkness and light,
   May in general be manifested in myriads of ways.
On the Mars, for instance, using the bright
   Solar rays and sets of mirrors, nights might be turned into
      days,

Virtually eliminating completely the condition of darkness.
   Compared to such a situation, our present earthly state
Is like that of medieval time here, when the candle's prowess
   Was all man had to combat darkness. Therefore, precipitate

This example and thousand others the way for the genuine
Scientist, so he can regard past theories and discoveries
Just as introduction. However, simple minds spin
And get readily tired at such thinking, or spending energy in
   these

Types of revelations, realizations, or pursuing anything
With care and perseverence; they care little to know!
Even then, the last thing we can say, the ultimate truth bring
Forth, about or through any discovery or any extensive row

Of discoveries, is merely one point out of an infinite
Aggregation of points, just one turn out of an infinite
Series of intersections and cross-roads the thinker might
Be able to see under a harmony with the Existence and the
   ensuing insight.

Likewise, an established scientific theory, however infallible,
   Is but one of endless forms and facets of the nature —
A mere point in the infinite continuum of evolution, visible
   As it emerges at the unison between the nature and the
      searcher.

The mind of the seeker, when in tune and harmony
   With the nature's evolutionary process at large —
In the depth of one's being, with ecstasy, no agony —
   Uncovers the pearl of truth, dark shell if able to discharge.

It's not only the eye of a Newton, or a Galileo, that perceived
  The passage and unfoldment of the pristine reality;
But it is the centrality of their inner selves that weaved —
  As crucial elements of their Godhead personality —

The panorama of the nature's intimate understanding.
  The discoveries aptly credited to their superior genius
Are indeed the works of their true inner being
  Which "sees", and really guides them to the infinite truth
    thus.

A naive individual, however, whose innate personality
  Has been lost into the maze of the daily strife
Is enveloped, engrossed, and enamored by it (what a pity!),
  Losing touch with the primal stability, the key to inner life.

To such a person the nature as well as the discoveries
  Of science appear as changeless, utterly stale;
In using them he simply reshuffles, reproduces with ease;
  And, with his creativity dormant, buried under a veil

Of ignorance, his thoughts acting like a calculating machine,
  A mechanical piston, he merely performs blind imitations
And rituals, feeding, as it were, as an unclean
  Parasite, on the toil and fruits of other men and nations.

Not a trace of their own being's knowledge
  They are able to present, nor to read in the book of the self.
Who knows why? May be because of their minds' erroneous
    ways
  And naively mistaking flickering images as the real look of
    the self.

***

The instance of a child starting his first school,
  And the very first lessons beginning with the alphabet

May be in order; for he would, as a rule,
  Learn them well, pronouncing his letters with zeal, thinking:
    yet

No one did learn them in a manner so fitting
  As he, or not at all before his adventurous mastery!
For example, I saw a child who, with a definite ring
  Of deep arrogance, asked me, "Have you studied biology?"

For, he had just heard the name of a book
  On biology, for the first time; and wouldn't miss the chance
To advertise his slick scholarship, while a mere ABC he mistook
  To be the end of learning—well, so much for an instance!

But the point is that as he grows, he'd likely construe
  And regard knowledge as a rigid, prespecified machinery,
And use it for self-defense, by design or in-promptu —
  Just as an attorney functioning in a framework or scenery

Of the established, extant laws—his thinking fully confined
  Within the inflexible bounds of the book of the prescribed
Law; unless he starts to explicate them, have them amended,
    redefined.
  Likewise, introductory lessons must be followed literally, as
    described.

If one day the mind of a novice should become
  Mature and well-versed and raise the query major:
"What's the use of learning, so far?"—he would hear a voice
    sum
  Up the answer—a voice of his conscience and living, innate
    nature —

And the answer would be—"For future objectives and gains!"
  However, wouldn't the future be but a repetition of the past —
A by-product of previous learning, fossilized remains?
  Then, free from the past's shadow would be no objective, no
    forecast.

The above is, clearly, a common experience: A person who just repeats
    The ideas of a scientist or a thinker turns not into that person;
A copy is never the original—someone reciting Keats
    Or Emerson or Hafez, with pomp, ranks not as Hafez, Keats
        or Emerson.

It's not quite uncommon, though, to see world-renowned
    Individuals repeating the words of great thinkers
And scholars, with little additions or facility, but crowned
    With their own name, proclaiming and exacting, acting as
        harbingers.

Standing before or confronting a receptive audience,
    They appear so forceful and arrogant, not perceiving
That, really, they've done, or are, nothing; and are, hence,
    Like stagnant, foul water, rather than a fresh, resourceful
        spring.

A person with collected, stored memory—details fully preserved—
    Is but akin to a mobile, silent little library.
On the contrary, whenever an inquisitive individual served
    The cause of knowledge, contemplating seriously

The knowledge of the past, the learning of scholars
    Preceding him—denoting a truly dynamic, innate,
Lively spirit in the researcher—that alone really ushers
    Results unprecedented: scientific, spiritual; man's future and
        fate.

—This the scientists call a vital, intimate, life-force,
    An inner inspiration, a revelation—but all that's nothing
But a harmonious intimacy that from the core pours
    To nourish the root connection of the inner self and the
        meaning

Of the outer manifestations and the sensual perceptions:
    A relation between the personality and the universe!

14

A supreme state of inspiration, then, really, placidly, runs
   Deep in the Existence; upwelling cognition as the seekers
      immerse!

And yet, the outcome of such a revelation and inspiration
   Bears little similarity with the results of the past;
Except, perhaps, a kinship of shared elemental relation
   Between a brand new theory that helps confirm the last,

Or a new law that negates the old one, by choice!
   However, the result of a true inspiration purely stands
On its very own, for the nature and the views and the voice
   Of a true personality with the discovery it solemnly bands.

A theory borne out of inspiration has its own distinguished
      root;
   And, when brought under comparative observations and
      analyses,
It's its proof in itself, bearing objectives and fruit,
   Ascent resonant with waves that pave the brain-cells as
      honey-bees.

As the great thinker, Bergson, also said before:
   Even the words of good writers or the performances of great
      actors
Can barely paint the personalities, whose presentations're made
      before
   An audience, the reason being two important factors:

First, for the lack of facts, of pieces of available information,
   Of full knowledge of the exact events, and so on and on,
A precise duplication is impossible; and secondly, still only a
      translation
   Of the original truth results, as the writers and playwrites don

Their own interpretations, and personalities, and nature,
   Consciously or subconsciously, by choice or just by default.

So, a discrepancy is inevitable between the truth and its
    caricature.
    A lack of harmony is the culprit in Bergson's truthful
      thought.

Thus, it's natural that many views people advance
    As the presentation of the same truth—some appearing true,
And some not so; and it's vital that we manage the chance
    Of independent thinking, with proper discrimination between
      the two:

Be it in the realm of purely scientific observations —
    Of the physics of natural events abounding around us,
Or a singular spiritual experience, of contemplations
    In the solitary depths of the Existence, of metaphysics—that
      found us!

What has been stated invariably loses its novelty —
    Even if it's the latest results; even if it's all crystal clear;
Even if it's for charting, marching on, or studying a trail—see,
    A future spiritual journey no past discovery can near.

At this point, however, I must explain a simple fact:
    Namely, the results of our sensual perceptions naturally face
The very same problem - for our senses do constantly write and
      act,
    Yet the true cognition escapes man—though full audition
      occupies the race.

***

To repeat, if one should bring to the stage the 'Socrates'
    Plato wrote, in an attempt to present to the audience
The real Socrates, the real Socrates will not still cease
    To defy transparent appearance, or pure, perfect credence.

None of the play-situations, or many a hypothetical point
    Will quite succeed in its skilled, intricate contrivance

16

In overcoming the void, the lack of meaning poignant
    Between the real and the make-belief—no matter which way
    we glance.

Even if the episodes in the play were in excellent harmony
    With the truth of Socrates' life, the scenes on the stage
Presented with utmost artistry will nevertheless suffer many
    Limitations, marring the identity of the two Socrates, at each
    phase!

For, that Socrates, the noble Greek, who lived in Athens
    Was a true being, in existence; while the play's just obsessed
With mere imitations of some remainder elements we sense
    To be of him, gathered by others—just a drama, a play at
    best!

In reality, Socrates' actual personality was his true essence;
    But in an attempt to capture it, the whole point is missed!
From the start, the comparison loses ground—as the present
    tense
    Can never be the past—and 'fore its start the play's finished!

The Socrates whose personality is like an unending stream
    From which truth emanates—a flame radiating brilliance,
Influencing everyone's mind and life—doesn't it seem
    Obvious that that great Socrates scarcely once sojourns

With the Socrates on the stage—a pet puppet in Plato's hands:
    Even though Plato toiled, under the gift of dedication
And faculty of a true student and an exposure from which one
    expands
    —So when Plato eyed Socrates, he saw but himself, else
    none!

In an analogy of the above, when the principal—that is, the self —
    Receives and incorporates what his sensual perceptions
    present;
He assumes, and is convinced, that those are there to help
    As true knowledge; not knowing that a greedy merchant

Of vested interests can rarely become a messenger
  Of the basic truth, especially of a spiritual character —
For he is forever an ignorant, confused, weary traveller,
  Unable to glimpse or grasp the reality's constant spur!

Maurice Maeterlinck, in his work: "The Great Secret",
  Describes beautifully his own sensual perception
Of a family, carrying crops, who sat to get
  A moment's respite, far in a distance, at a little elevation,

By their meandering meadow—a pretty picture indeed!
  —But, while the picture is manifested in the beholder's eyes,
It also cognitively depicts (or, truly tries to lead)
  The viewer's inner state—with an aim to surmise

The reality; so in a way, with due construction and emotion,
  — the viewer himself gives finishing touches to its goal.
This simile, in fact, bears significant psychological notion:
  Sensual perception reflects the viewer's state of heart and
    soul.

In essence, the external images bearing gross physical events
  Subtly embody the viewer's mental capability and spiritual
    state.
The inner eyes' color filters what the canvas bears in paints;
  And each message you're reading now is on your own mental
    slate.

Thus the sensual perception and the internal interpretation
  Far outweigh the occurrences lying in the outer world!
For example, a beautiful garden with a specific conglomeration
  Of characteristics, at a given time, would be apparently
    unfurled

Differently to different people, depending on their own inner
    state:
  A convict condemned to the gallow; or committed to prison
    for life;

Or a poet in love, ecstatically involved, will all naturally relate —
  As would a child, or a sick person—to it differently, by their
    type.

It is thus impossible that an external observation
  Doesn't unravel the gallery of one's own stored memory,
Or toss leaves as the wind, set dust in stray motion,
  Or paint meanings colored by the moment's pert story.

In so far as man's sensual and mental states
  Interfere with manifestations and interpretations of events,
It's virtually impossible that the ultimate reality penetrates
  His consciousness freely and purely; for his animal self
    presents

Him—through his sensual perception—with crippled, impaired
    images,
  Screened through the lenses of his current inner state:
Well, this may be skilled viewing, like photographing, or
    reading pages;
  But to call it the *reality* or true knowledge is to over-rate.

True knowledge is, certainly, as was said before,
  Free of any uncertainty, redundancy, or relativity.
Such inner knowledge emanates and springs from the core,
  Imparting understanding from metaphysical means, and
    purity.

So, we'll refer to the above type of knowledge as 'true', or
    'innate';
  And call sensual perception 'acquired knowledge', to
    differentiate.

***

19

Existence is the subject of a mysterious fate —
In a riddle-like fashion—apparently without meaning!
An individual entity: be it a speck of dust,
Or a human being—seems to have little free will in it!

In reality, everything is utterly dependent on, and a microstate
of, a Universal Grand Existence, a Supreme Being,
Encompassing the boundless universe; each particle is an entity
*   just*
Limited completely if seen through the rather limited slit

Of the lens of man; but the Gate
Of Existence offers a view quite unlimited, all-encompassing!
And so each individual entity is—as it must
Be—free, being a parcel of the free totality, sans limit.

***

The reflection of the sun's rays here on the earth,
And in the infinite universe, is indeed the reflection
Of the invisible and undetected electromagnetic waves,
Manifesting as light only at their destination.

And under this light, the days here on the earth,
With all their happenings in every direction,
Must appear from another planet as it likely behaves
And appears to us at night, as it reflects the illuminating sun.

Powerful gravitational waves from one planet to another
Draw and hold them together, and control their motion.

Not a speck of dust is beyond, or free from, their hold;
Not a trace of space is outside their all pervading influence.

Even reckoning this, when we view the heaven's treasure,
Glittering on a clear night, we get the notion:
That each planet, satellite or star—all gems, silver and gold —
Is on its own free course, without interactions, with full
    independence.

From the tiny pebble off-shore to the ocean as a whole,
The Milky Way ov'rhead to trillions of globular clusters,
And mammoth groups of galaxies, and splendid starry beaches
And the ocean of the space—at each point of the skies,

Fierce and grand waves are constantly at play, their role
Being to guide each body as it dashes, or spins, or stirs,
Or swings in suspension to space's farthest ever reaches,
Under knowledgeable, calculable and measurable laws precise.

But strangely enough the workings of the nature and the
    universe
(Our own abode from the moment we breathe first to the last!) —
We seem to have forgotten, or to take too much for granted!
The pulsing force of the creation seems silently absent from it all.

If a small particle is disturbed from its journey, of course it
    alters
The destiny of the natural manifestations, as they go past
Unknown milestones, new destinations—such hidden
    knowledge planted
And enshrined is in the nature, even if not within man's call, or
    recall.

How can these exact and ordered natural phenomena —
That follow a precise path of knowledge in the universe —

Be comprehensible to an earthly being like man?
Man's sensory perceptions and the greatest poetic imagination

Are far too weak, inadequate instrumentations or antenna
To capture from the arena the ins and outs of, what particles
And waves, in their dual dance, dexterously can
Continually present, and cast from the past to the future
        presentation.

However, it is rather simply difficult to accept
That the order of the planets and the universe doesn't affect
My life and my living, my thoughts and my imagination,
And, ultimately, the tiniest, and entire, aspect of my being.

How can one accept that, in mind having kept
That something coming from the nature's womb is, naturally,
        subject
To be possessed by the nature, and to reflect it, to each
        respiration,
To the very core, including my living, my thinking, my seeing?

Having come this far, at this phase of this infinitely long
Journey, it'd be strange that the nature's influence —
Exitence's express pressure—now ceases to exist!
Indeed I'm but just a culmination of the entire

Evolutionary unfolding phenomena—a constant cosmic song
And a wonderous cosmic dance of the universal nature in
        progress!
To wish to defy this is being an extremist
In adolescence of the mind, in juvenile delinquency dire.

***

In my opinion, the nature is a competent teacher,
And a capable master: in bringing miniscule particles and rays
To their ultimate destinies, it commits errors none;
Even the most formidable barriers fail to alter its course.

And so well predetermined and independent fixed feature
Of invariant strict regulation and guidance it displays —
That little freedom is left to anything or anyone;
The power I employ stems from only a natural source.

But ignorant of this fact—that only the nature endows
Power and dignity to me—for lack of appropriate references,
I mistake these as mine, and independence and free-will too;
As if the nature gave us thus gifts it does not itself possess!

Surely some logical, intellectual and sensory reasons and vows
Could undo this presumptuous error from our frame and
    senses. Each inch of the earth endures—from the valley to the
    peak, hill to
The alley's dust—the pressure the atmosphere commonly
    impresses.

***

Man's utter folly (regarding himself above all)
And arguments that negate free will can be easily refuted
By simple logical reasoning: as typified, for instance,
By the case of the atmospheric pressure—outlined below.

In 1631, Descartes introduced the idea novel
Of vacuum; and Evangelista Torricelli then computed,
Based on Vincent Vioyani's experimental stance
With glass pipes of mercury, in 1643, the weight 0'

A mercury column of one square centimeter, 76 centimeters in
    height,
Thereby explaining the air pressure always exerted
On every point of the earth. Therefore, in accordance
With this observation, from the moment materials arrive

In a corporeal form, they're subjected to this airy might
Of the atmosphere, and adjust to this process. No one is
    exempted

From this law of the nature, this force from above, this
     obeisance.
This natural effect, an acute governing factor of human life,

Has a complete influence on man's well-being.
And even though this effect is observable, and frightening
In proportion, even in imagination, man is hardly given
To a moment's thought or concern about this enormous force!

Not even once to his notice does he bring
This natural constraint he must obey, without knowing It.
Let's think of the moon that follows every direction
Of the earth, following and orbiting around it constantly, of
     course.

Still the moon, the small earthly satellite, does have a great
Influence on the earth. Its movements make great waves
In the waters of the oceans and seas; and without doubt the
     earth
And its inhabitants are affected by these lunar conditions.

How, then, could man not be influenced by, his fate
Not have a bearing, on such conditions? Or how he behaves
Could not carry their mark? From the very birth
Physically and mentally, man's behavior, thought and dictions

Must reflect these influences. After all, how is man,
A finite being and almost a vanishing body compared with
The infinite universe, worthy or capable of possessing a free
     will?
(The dependency and vulnerability of man on nature is self-
     evident)

The reflections of orbital gravitations on capable minds can
Shape their course; even though invisible, these forces lie
     beneath
Each move of our perceptible minds; for the gravitational mill
And other natural sources emit waves that, to some extent,

Determine the fate of all in their wake—certainly no less
Our susceptible minds than the brilliant stars, the earth, the sun.
If our hearing were to be more stable and capable
Of perceiving more accurately, we could follow the echoes

Of the sublime thoughts in the very deep recesses
Of Newton's and Kepler's sky, as well as orbital gravitation.
Their validity relates to something independent, to a stable
Existence; the existence of a general rational system it surely
    shows.

If the orbital gravitation leads the orbital planets,
Is it so strange to suppose that the universal mind should lead
To the spirituality of the planet's intelligent inhabitants?
And a proportionality or balance in the spiritual and physical

Systems leads the mind of man, which then gets
The ability to recognize invisible truths under the germane seed
Of the influence from the physical and metaphysical chants
Or the nature's waves—thus progresses the evolution universal.

Similarly an inherent binding the nature exerts over me.
With no say in it, obey and follow it fully, I must!
This natural effect indeed may be a factor of great import,
Impacting my well-being, my health, my existence, my very life-
    course.

And although this natural influence I could feel, imagine, or
    see;
Still, to me, withstanding this pressure is an unbearable thrust.
We witness it profusely, on life's long course, as on escort;
But we rarely even think of, or acknowledge, this grand life-
    force:

As if the order of destination, the predetermination is
    surrendered
To, and accepted so-so, as a rule; though quite tacitly.
And this order holds reciprocally, so no one is really free!
A universal interdependence and predetermination thus results.

For instance, the moon—a baby in the sun's family—is
    rendered
To go round the mother earth under its gravity, quite placidly;
But the moon's magic makes seven oceans dance in spree?
And who knows—my own fate might bear the lunar catapults!

Such is the predicament of the earth and its inhabitant:
And throughout this universe, there is continual give and take.
None of us is immune from this omnipresent flux
Of circle of influences that rule, and control, and supervise.

In any case, the thoughts of man are so very scant
And limited in the universe unlimited—they'd hardly make or
    break
The nature's day, or order; but if one's ready brain lucks
An incidence of the nature's waves—it's like daybreak at the
    sunrise!

***

If our senses should develop the capability to receive
More intricate, fine phenomena; then the subtle and sublime
    realms
Of the superior order of thoughts and the metaphysical world
Would appear as substantial as the ocean waves!

Then the credibility of the "supernatural" occurrences we'll
    achieve,
Taking them as simple results—as the sages' inspired psalms —
Of a higher rational order; and if the gravity universally twirled
Each planet's course, wouldn't that a universal spirit paves,

As a guiding force invisible, each spiritual being's path?
A common unified field of the nature's spirit and man's
Might envelope this earth, and all planets that might exist
With inhabitants evolved to obtain a greater order of intellect!

Intellectual discoveries are spurred, like an 'Eureka' in the bath,
Like a bright flash in the brain, like a lightning that instantly
    scans
The sky down to the earth—such revelations necessarily enlist
A harmony, for the mind to cognize the nature's deep secret:

A harmony between the physical and the metaphysical elements
    involved
Of the person's whole being, between the discoverer and the
    nature itself;
A harmony that feeds the brain, making it more fertile,
And aptly capable for the synthesis by the nature's waves great!

This harmony at this point results in the intrinsic problem
    solved —
As the metaphysical wave resonates and imprints its message to
    help
The thinker, entering his intellect through the third channel, in a
    while
Dissolving the physical distance his sensual perceptions create.

In realizing the nature's truth, cognizing the deep correlation
Between the Existence and his being, physicality and
    spirituality,
He discovers one of the theoretical principles and scientific
    laws;
And in bringing about a true harmony and union between the
    universe

And his senses and his brains, his consciousness and his
  observation
Of the nature, his inner self and the true character and quality
Of the external world—he conceives the laws, and benevolently
  draws
And signs his intellectual will to mankind, its validity confirms.

Obviously, the significance, depth, strength, or life
Of the law, or of all such intellectual contributions, indeed,
Is directly proportional to the degree of harmony
Between his being and the nature and Existence as a whole.

[Thus, achieving this harmony is the essence of the strife
That underlies a scientific and intellectual feat and deed
Of superior caliber—which, by the way, is no irony;
Since science and spirituality really share the same goal.]

***

Joseph Cenil writes that the way he perceived
The Sixth Sense is through the realization of magnetic waves,
Whose field resembles the astral body—so subtle
They pass through everything, and need no natural elements to
  be bred.

When, with the Sixth Sense, control is well achieved -
By a person ov'r his mind, or a part thereof, it saves
The day; for then he can win therefrom any obstacle,
And gainfully invoke the harmony with the field invested.

This simply enhances the mind's susceptibility;
Eliminating the 'static noise', he can prepare and then succeed
In tuning into any given station, loud and clear,
And get the signal extracted from the respective carrier wave.

The harmony waves the wand and the hat generates new
   visibility;
Newton's law of gravity, and discoveries of the like creed,
Are barely glimpses and signs of the vast scenarios of the shear
Reality of greatest power and interchanges that's Existence's
   slave.

To creatures a type of magnetism the nature did attach;
And we shall view the laws of this animal magnetism
Later; but what Joseph Cenil meant is this:
A clairvoyant person is one who, having controlled

Fully well at least a part of his brain, can catch
The natural external magnetic waves in synergism.
By this indeed is referred a harmony—like a bliss —
A coherence between the physical and the spiritual powers
   untold.

A superior harmony and coherence of the physical and spiritual
   forces
With the existing universal forces and powers, lead to great
Miracles, as then the mind is ready and capable to tune
Into the entire spectrum of waves, and the voice of God!

Although precise scientific and spiritual laws one endorses
Based suitably on observations and experiments, a straight
Realization of the truth takes place in the laboratory of mind,
   the tribune
Or the messenger effective is a universal intelligence to lead or
   prod.

Just as a transmitter or receiver can transmit or receive properly
Only under suitable conditions—the same applies
For reception of universal waves or intelligence supreme, divine.
The insensitive, untuned, or deaf miss, the broadcast colossal.

The space we inhabit is immersed in vibrant life surely —
From the heart of the atom to the endless intergalactic skies —
With physical and metaphysical events, but even if we be an
    Einstein,
Our knowledge of them is meager; our physical and spiritual
    make-up dull.

Our present constitution is not a-priori capable
Of discerning the inherent meaning and the latent deep mystery.
But the essential thing is to be in close harmony
And in unison with the nature—all aspects of the Existence.

For instance, being in unison, on the same level, we're able
To see and hear, with our visionary and auditory machinery,
Receiving the light and sound waves, when these pose harmony;
While the rest of the spectrum out of phase, makes no sense.

Even so, what we see and hear is taken as reality
Only by comparison and relativity; but is it truly real?
It is distinct from the reality of the absolute, perennial laws
Of Existence, as the sensual organs' functions are so lame,

Operative in such limited domains, whereas to glimpse a part of
    the infinity
That's the absolute reality, we need a blessed power, perception
    integral.
The closer to the infinite reality one gradually draws,
The more one assumes oneself true aspects of the same.

To grasp any concept that its mark on nature imprints,
To develop and to expand up to it, dissolving all boundaries,
An interaction has to evolve, a relationship well established,
With love of, and dedication to, the knowledge involved.

An infinite exchange is the very first condition, the very first
    hints
In this sublime process; sensual perception, with frail limits and
    worries,
Can never uncover and illuminate the reality, or herald its gist;
Sensual perception alone can merit no great discoveries or
    riddles solved.

The far-sighted seers, the noble-minded thinkers of the East
Have definitely come upon this fateful belief, this factual
    realization—
That if all the sensual, mental and other faculties of man
Are focussed on to discovering a higher set of truths, more
    refine

Than their habitual animal tendencies and desires that exist
Continually, pulling him down; then only, through their
    sublimation,
Can he receive those waves with precision and sensitivity that
    can
Help unveil nature's laws, that we've as metaphysical
    underlined.

Under such sublimation of the sensual perceptions, and true
    concentration,
Man's secretly enshrined, innate power comes to stand
At his beck and call, under his full control and command
Of his higher intelligence—mirroring, spelling the world's
    happenings.

And then is man able, in proportion of his consciousness's
    consecration,
To harness that energy, in resonant excellence over the nature's
    waves grand
That adorn the realm of divinity—each ray of nature a wand —
And bring to existence all objects, the universe, himself, all
    beings.

He is presently unable to detect these waves;
For, true cognition appears only when one transcends
The outward appearance, to grasp the meaning within.
And when the impulse and the intellect, the senses and the spirit

Strive in true harmony, by notes and by octaves,
With the Existence's manifestation, then one's personality tends
To be guided by the nature's ultimate elements pristine —
A characteristic that makes one ascend to the spiritual summit.

The essence of this grand scheme is presented in the instance
And form of a Man who's a unique, perfect model
And spiritual master to the species—a gift the nature bestows
In every age, and land—to symbolize, as it were,

The true meaning of God's Viceregency, an emissary of human
    penance —
To encourage mankind—as great sages did show and tell;
On the contrary, the fragmentation and disarray a predisposed
    mind shows
Of the natural powers, prevent the perception of the nature's
    fine texture.

Such a disturbed mind, for all that matters, is no better
Than the dismantled and useless machine with parts engaged
In doing different things incoherently, with little coordination
    or focus.
People with such mental state cannot, or are not able to, act

For performance of deeds, or self-expression, or even to just
    take care
Of themselves or their affairs; for they see not the play being
    staged
Within their view, nor the truth omnipresent; their constant
    little fuss
Or fruitless shallow deeds are no measure of man's master tract.

***

A true and noble society is keenly responsible
To promote sciences and other fields of learning,
And to encourage scientists and others with a yearning
For the pursuit of knowledge
(lest progress should become impossible).

***

What transpires when electromagnetic waves sprint —
Universal, infinite, precisely ordered and structured
Entity coming in contact, in real time, with the brain-cells
   nurtured
By an alert and reflective mind, leaving its imprint?

The interaction between the two fields then definitely leads
The mind to the discovery of the secrets of the nature;
Or, when certain scientific accidents, as it were, occur,
They bring forth new theories that sow new seeds

Of knowledge, opening new frontiers for the present
And future generations and civilizations.
Inevitably, the appropriate declarations and publications
Would follow, provided in worthiness endures the content.

At the beginning, no matter how insignificant such an accident
May appear, it would receive the highest acclaim in no time,
And would benefit, and be employed by, the world in the prime;
For, a raw seed barely grows to bear fruit latent.

Yet many a precious and worthy thoughts and views
Do remain buried and obscure, as rays behind a cloud;

As fire wears smoke and ashes, like a curtain or a shroud.
And lacking substance or appreciation, the news

Of such a discovery remains, indeed, a news
Only to its despairing discoverer, all alone.
Such a gift, then, deprived of expression, failure-prone,
Would wait, and finally ascend back to the eternity; and we lose

It for ever, as the thinker or discoverer passes away.
For instance, Gauss, the famous German mathematician,
    credited with 146
Mathematical contributions, and that particular mix
Of brilliant brain-cells, might not have been known today —

Had it not been for the patronage of Duke de Bernscheveich!
Similarly, as written in Augustin Kuchi's biography,
The society would have missed the torch and the trophy
Of his glorious contributions, but for King Louis XVIII's
    patronage rich.

For the realization of any scientific advancement,
Of course, suitable conditions and the essential means
Must be provided; the spring of knowledge a channel of word
    weans.
The result expected would be improbable, if that were not
    present.

If one pays attention to the history of nations,
It would be apparent that the most advanced countries
Or civilizations have announced the latest discoveries.
However, except for a general lack of public support and
    publications,

Even less advanced countries have their fair share
Of great men, scientific ideas and philosophical contributions;
The harbingers of knowledge land every port, everywhere talent
    runs.
For propagation of knowledge, no one is a sole heir.

Yet, the advanced countries definitely do provide
A greater level of support and stimulation to the process,
A greater appreciation to the value of discoveries, not less.
And, in turn, these discoveries benefit those countries in stride.

***

It is unfortunate that almost in every society,
The indifferent, idle, self-centered, pseudo-intellectual
Elements and modes often by far outstrip many a true
　　individual
Given to the service of science, and arts, and goodness, and
　　piety.

It has been so always, and so it is at the moment.
A true man of high learning is invariably in a small minority.
And whenever they endeavor to advance ideas bearing quality,
And novelty, and the promise of mankind's benefit, and good
　　intent,

They are immediately faced with the weapons of prejudices,
Superstitions, and even direct threat to their interest and being.
Many a discovery and publication of new laws may be seeing
The graveyard dust as it is buried in books in libraries' recesses,

Losing the slightest chance to fall on the fertile
Grounds of public awareness, to reveal their true essence;
This is why the works of great people bear credence
Mainly to true students, the seekers of truth, without rank and
　　file.

And if, perchance, the seekers and the thinkers went
By virtue of their innate nature, without hesitation,
To the extent of laying their lives in the celebration
Of truth, their fate may get fatally spent

In prosecution by the clergy or others, subject to the accusation
Ludicrous and outrageous—Galileo and Socrates

Stood trial for giving utterance to truths one now sees
As self-evident as the sun, embracing death and condemnation.

I wish that the essence of the intellect
Would be the illumined standard for the mind
Of common people; so neither would illusion find
Any room, nor ignorance-based irrevocable action be the
   circumspect,

Thereby guarding against such ill-fated occurrences.
The truly enlightened thinkers of any culture, indeed,
Are the forerunners of the achievements of civilization; the
   wonderous seed
Is sown by them, and the harvest of prosperity for their
   followers well commences.

***

There are many who criticize devoted scientists
For not introducing and describing their discoveries
To the common populace, as a favour, but the fact is
That ordinary people might judge, as history amply lists,

The scientific findings by their very incomplete
Thoughts and ideas, ridiculing them, destroying
The scientist's very life. It's awkward, however, to think
Of a scientist as a merchant who must elaborately beat

The drum of his merchandise and supplies and services,
Despite the ill-conditions, society's aimless envy.
To face the society's folly is the gross, inevitable levy
The scientist but must pay, and continue his own researches

To fruition in time, ultimately, till success fortunately smiles,
And his life as a scientist, sort-of, attains ascension,
While the people's folly falls—needless it's to mention —
As the worthless query dies that expectation odd beguiles.

In his autobiography, Dr. Mesmer, the founder of the theory
Of hypnotism, refers to the many unkindnesses of
The society, alluding to his own ill-treatment, scoff
In the society's hand, with many of the details gory:

He was not given the chance to live in his own
City and to continue research; but was, instead, forced
To live in the village of Fro Angeld in Switzerland, coerced
By the conditions to make his living as a doctor, unknown

To the people for his true field and great genius;
Still he continued his research in his free
Time on hypnotism (as well as on healing) as primary
Mission of his life, knowledge being his prime impetus.

As evidenced by his letter to Berlin Academy,
Where he was invited (after all these atrocities
Committed on him), he said—his words a release
Of the sadness and profound grief on his ill-fated infamy —

That he was willing to spend the rest of his life
In a corner away from the trials, not inviting
Any more troubles from people, rather than go on fighting
Which, unfortunately, already claimed the best of his life.

At another invitation extended to him later
By Professor Welfart, he said, "The sun
Of my life already traversed down the horizon.
Not much is left of it, and I've no greater

Wish than to spend the remaining rays
And time therein in the study of that
Discipline that's my heart's real inhabitat,
And that I've come to know in many ways

To be beneficial. In this way, I hope
That at the end of my life I may obtain
Some useful results, and my whole life in vain
Wouldn't be; I'd have weaned for what now I grope."

The history of humanity knows of no true scientist,
Who travelled the road of knowledge with a view to gain riches;
Fame, possessions, wealth are not quite his niches;
These are childish urges to him, not his thought's or invention's
    gist.

Conceit-based logic whose concept and reasoning is based
On egotism and self-praise, ignorance and conceit,
Is seldom a basis of a fine culture, a great civilization's seat;
Rather, a conceit-based concept is no logic—it must be faced.

Immediate financial gains blinded not the mentor's vision,
Nor blurred with myopia the master's eye-sight.
The chairs in the centers of learning, however, bear ironic plight
As they are filled with men of empty words, not of worthy
    mission.

But for their efforts, people's minds would wallow even more
In selfish thoughts and mundane acts and deprivations.
Their contributions lend strength to the lands and civilizations,
In tune with spiritual light, heightening true happiness each
    shore.

That the wise must bear the burden of the ignorant —
Is a great pity; it's the gravest injustice they endure.
What a shame the society cares not to make sure
To encourage and comfort, in time, the brave and the elegant

And the sensitive souls of its thinkers and creators!
The lives of many ill-fated scientists in the society
Are testimony to this sad plight: Take, for instance, the story
Of Kalway, to whose soul people acted just like traitors.

The father of the Group Theory led a singularly solitary life,
Full of utter misery and hardship supreme!
And yet, principled, to responsibly preserve his life's creme,
His knowledge, for the world and the humanity, the strife

He wore; and as he lay on his death-bed, he willed on a page
Or two, a succinct summary of what he knew, the torch to
   pass on,
As his breath ebbed as the dwindling candle's flicker by morn,
Not seeing the dawn, but vanishing for ever in a thin smokey
   image!

What horrible hardships and callous calamities he charted
While living! What dark dreadful pangs of a difficult death
   he had!
But, alas! though often the sages and scientists face such sad
Misfortune, does it awaken the slumbering souls of the stone-
   hearted

People? In fact, that is *the* paramount misfortune
And incalculable loss to the humanity at large:
That such a lot should befall the ship and the barge
And the captain trading in knowledge—its vistas and its boon.

***

The true personality of a nation is doubtlessly dependent
On the scientific achievements that its people represent.
And science is not merely a repetition of the past and the present
Knowledge; but true scientific achievement should be primarily
   meant

To open true avenues for the future's life, purposefully
   directed,
To lead to the discoveries of yet more momentous mysteries,
To harmonize the land of intellect with the spirit's soaring seas —
To pass through the gate, to enter the City of Knowledge,
   subjected

To, and perfected by, the touch of the Absolute Ruler's glance!
To bring forth and breathe in a spiritual civilization serene

(Then, each heart is the reflection of the heavenly kingdom's
  scene;
And salvation would come to man, as on completing the
  penance).

***

Throughout the world, extensive abundance of talent
Exists in the society; indeed, in every country and land!
But in the underdeveloped countries, as it were, talent is banned
— As the doors of centers of learning, of universities eminent,

Are closed to individuals of creativity in fields
Ranging from science to spirituality, even to artisans
And craftsmen innovative, able to develop new solutions
And methods to reform, technique that rebuilds.

Unfortunately, however, a university that does not
Encourage and foster innovative and positive thinking,
Is no more than a public library, an elevated utility building!
Recitation of books is all right; but what matters is the process
  of thought.

***

This treatise is not to be considered poetic at all;
For, it dwells on, and deals in, the core of pure reality.
Thus, even if we consider the purpose of knowledge, without
  ambiguity,
To be to move the wheels of commerce, to be at matter's beck
  and call,

For just earthly services of the people, under the supervision
Of experienced scientists; even then the value of the outcome
Of such a scientific endeavor or mission displays a spectrum
Far wider than a mine (be it of gold), or an agricultural
  institution.

Even the wheels of commerce run smoother when fueled and
   lubricated
By science's innovations, by the far-sighted thoughts of true
   men of science
This, in fact, is the significant solution to invoke time
And again, for the betterment of the world's economic plight
   emaciated.

***

What is undoubtedly evident is that those individuals
Who do not use their mental faculty, spurred with the quest of
   the spirit,
Shaped by thought's centrality unified with God, deserve no
   credit.
They are, for all that matters, mentally bankrupt, insane to their
   skulls.

Devoid of a unifying Godly spirit, a centrality, they are burdens
To the society, feeding on its vitality, like parasites.
Universities should, then, safeguard the society's inner lights,
Acting as the center of ingenuity, spirit and sense.

Failing in this true mission, a university surely degenerates
Into a body without the mind, a head without the nerve-cells.
No matter what set of actions and transactions it busily dwells
In, it is only the society's sickness and death it inculcates.

On the contrary, if a university should be enthusiastic,
   conducive,
And vitally active toward the development and nurturing of
   novel
Science and thoughts and ideas, as a mother wishing well
Of the foetus, then the scientist will warmly embrace it, and
   himself give.

I have also come across talented individuals—I must mention —
In my society, who've had enthusiasm and devotion;

43

And the will to gain knowledge, crossing the dark ocean
Of ignorance of centuries, to know the latest invention;

So that they do not end up re-inventing the wheel;
Or, committing an error for lack of touch with the past works.
But, admittedly, in my consciousness this regret today lurks
That, unfortunately, I've been unable to be their guide and
    counsel.

***

The publication of one or more scientific newspaper ought to
    be free
For the public, so as to serve as a channel to speak on science.
The influence of such a factor on the receptive minds
Is so immense, it can't but must be considered most seriously.

For illumination and guidance of seriously-minded individuals
Toward their scientific destiny, it could be the simplest
Way, to make the searching mind hopeful, to ensure that its
    quest
Will win success, and to have glimpses from the spirit's high
    citadels.

The spiritual aspirations of every human being
Is directed toward lofty and noble achievements;
If the spark of life shines in every environment (all saints
And the scientists shall excell, and their good fortune will sing)

Then, despite the conspiracy of the evil-minded people,
The ill-fates of the wise would be automatically vanquished.
Civilizations will attain its brilliant glory distinguished —
The wise shall build future civilizations, overcoming each
    obstacle.

***

If we shan't straighten and rectify
our outer appearance
and our inner selves,
the picture of our past days
will be most freightening, and painful instance
of existence, an unbearable and shameful far cry!

***

A physicist describes a wave
by explaining the effect of dropping a pebble —
undulations propagating from the center
to the edge of the body of water!
The wave is seen as a motion of unstable
points in the medium that behaves
in a certain pattern under transmission
of various after-effects or specific transformations.

If you put a smoked glass-plating
in front of your eyes, and observe,
the sun, radiating and irradiating,
and view the light ray refracting through it,
it acts as a handy diffraction grating
to show a set of concentric rings
of the seven rainbow colors—the ones originating
in the sun, and vividly creating
the two basic forms in their transit —
namely, illumination and darkness,
shadows and shinings,
not unlike the contrast the water waves serve.

Common to each wave-like structure
is propagation of sinusoidal vibration pattern
of the fluctuation of a field, consisting
of numerous crests and troughs —
the positive and negative extremes of vibration.
Such a simple vibration pattern
is common and inevitable in, and essential representation
of, every level of the nature —
They are the general expression
of the natural structure
which philosophers, such as Descartes,
characterized and labelled
as the indivisible ultimate unit,
the elementary constituent entity,
the atom of the matter.
In fact, as the scientists and students
of the modern quantum theory know well,
the elementary particles
and the fundamental ingredients
of all matter—electrons, leptons,
photons, protons, neutrons, atoms, molecules,
and the basic composites thereof,
possess a sort of dual nature,
an inherent ambiguity of character;
for, they behave as ordinary particles
as well as waves, undulations.
Even vast expanses of matter,
such as galaxies and their superclusters
and mammoth organised assemblies
of celestial bodies
of the universe
exhibit
characteristics and movements
that symbolize nature that apparently represents
an infinite sequel of images
like a movie, and eloquently stages
its endless play, in prose and in verse.

So, the nature invariably displays
infinite wave-forms, contracting and expanding
at every point, at every instant giving
birth to form that as particle behaves;
and the nature lives
in duality
of particles and waves.

***

The natural duality of waves and particles
naturally appears to hold logic subtle
in relation to the fundamental unity —
an inherent oneness—within the diversity
of existence in the universe throughout.
It is the oneness of the image
of the Absolute Existence, of God,
with the power of the physical
and metaphysical forces
and forms of the nature at large.
This analogy is not to deny the reality
of the existence of matter, or the material world,
or to suggest that the nature's significance is less.
But we should know the matter's play
as essentially an appearance,
and recognize the existence
of superior powers, especial forces -
beyond the grasp of the limited intellect,
beyond the scope of the fragile oscilloscope
of our life-time
research, observation, and realization
that constitute the 'ultimate truths' tangible to us.
These forces that lose
their form and dimension in the infinity,
and thereby remain
an inexhaustible riddle to us,
are, indeed, the ultimate reality.

If you note this as the truth,
the 'real' world
of matter and sensual perception
takes different sensual forms
in time due to certain interconnecting reasons,
due to certain interactions;
but they have not lost their connection
with the infinite!

***

As noted by Helmholtz, ultimately,
one must come to the realization
that the important task of physics is to relate
the basis of the appearance of the nature
with the power of the family of interactions
— the various classes of attractions and repulsions —
with the distance as the crucial parameter
governing the intensity of interaction,
the magnitude of the action and reaction.
The nature being based
on a constant solid foundation
the secret of the nature will be known
and the seeds of true knowledge fruitfully sown,
when the above types of relationships
are fully understood.
And yet, such relationships serve at best
merely to expose the external forms, appearances.
So, though, conventionally,
science would have achieved its task,
the true task remains far from complete.
If Helmholtz were to put forward a larger
truth, he would say science has taken
only a first step in its discovery
of the absolute truth, the paramount perennial reality,
which, up to this time, has been only
stated through reasoning, presented through logic.
From then on, for sure, the reasoning

and the logic would be more real, living,
for proving the reality of Existence
and for explaining the nature of the nature
by the emissaries and propounders
of different philosophies and laws.
In any event, the various
series of waves mentioned earlier
have only temporary modes;
of different philosophies and laws.
In any event, the various
series of waves mentioned earlier
have only temporary modes;
for, after certain systematically observed
regular actions and reactions, episodes,
they invariably suffer variation of form and codes,
undergoing a definite transformation of status.

If it were possible for a viewer to stand
at a point in a wave of his own course
of natural life and to be constant
and stable at that point, and if he could
view this wave from the past and
to the future—with all the events
of his life drawn on it,
he would see with his conscious
and subconscious mind, to the extent
of his visionary capability,
his total past, his entire future,
like an unending bountiful book.

This interpretation of our perspective
relative to time is not unrealistic;
because the essential gist of human spirit
and sacramental soul is akin to the
fourth dimension of physics,
but out of control
or confines of all the four
dimensions of space and time.

**

The human soul is not confined
to the boundaries of space and time.
From the perspective of the stages
beneath it, all the forms of barriers
are subject to the definite
limitations of space and time,
and therefore
of vision —
a situation
not too unlike
the case of an ant travelling
between two points a short distance a ... part.
For example, imagine that an ant
is travelling from point A to point B
in ten minutes; the ant itself
is passing according
to the unit of its step, is taking
ten minutes to go
from A to B, while an observer like us
sees the whole distance in no time.
The case of the ant versus
us
is basically quite similar
to the case of our bodies
versus our souls,
our real selves.
Extrasensory perception, clairvoyance,
dreams and inspiration
that come true—all undoubtedly serve
to show the power souls
possess, as superior viewers
unfettered by time, unhampered by space,
unlike the body's case.
In the life-history of man
or of any other being,
for that matter,
all of nature is just like
an infinite rich scroll,

on which all the events and occurrences
are recorded, as a story whole.
Or, the nature could be compared to
an infinitely long film-roll,
on which each event is depicted
without fail, which, in turn,
provides natural manifestation
of the world of nature
through the ages.

***

The above picturization
clearly leads to the principle of fate,
of predestination,
where the absolute will
leads to the explanation
of existence
as stemming from, and having intimate
relation with, all infinite Existence,
as the image of a candle in the mirror.

Considering the above explanations,
neither the true events of our lives,
nor their natural manifestations
are futile, or mere fairy-tale-like.
The present state of ours is rooted
in a constant and stable source,
where all the past and future
events are engraved, so to say;
all latent phases
of our passing days,
our daily and lifelong passages
encoded in immutable letters.

If scientists were to opine
that the present condition of every being
is the effect of the past history

51

in a summary manner,
then it would definitely not matter at all
if we were to adopt the following proposition —
In spite
of the blatantly incongruent
display of past and present,
cause and effect, matter and force,
we would not separate the original
appearance of any being whatsoever
from its extant situation or imposter.
We should rather laboriously discover
the linkage between its past, the certain source
of its current existence, and this current.
Existence is like an unbroken thread representing various
   reflections and inflexions of the past,
each individual event
unique,
without losing its continuous connection with the infinite.

Instead
of getting lost and bewildered in separate identity of things,
we must view their integral
interrelationships and significance.
If we consider,
the construction of a television
set and its astounding ability
of processing the endless set of images
and their interplay toward reproduction
of scenes and events and occurrences;
of transmission and reception
of an ad-hoc arbitrary signal,
of weaving the waves into picture after picture
meaningful and coherent,
of capitalizing an ascent and descent
of waves to create fleeting daily vision
of lasting, immaculate monument
of life and the world in motion —
then we may come to the recognition

that this is not too dissimilar
to our own superficial
psychic predisposition,
man's common mental state, of course.
And as the myriad of images on the screen
invariably derive their origins
from electromagnetic waves of singular, homogeneous
    characteristics,
so also—one can forward the assumption and projection
that—for every entity or being in the universe,
a singular grand origin continuously spins
its existence, like a continuous endless thread.
If we look at the television system,
the camera, transferring its image-static wave
from one state to another,
from a motion picture to electromagnetic waves
travelling from one station or point to the same station,
in the fashion of an ascending and descending curve, our
reasoning is proven to be correct
and the laws of the returning
to the origin is acceptable
in all of our studies,
in all the letters writ
and read.

***

Therefore,
in summary,
one may conclude
that all beings, after having gone through
their fated course of life, leave their imprints,
like images on the frame, marks on the mould,
in this continuous moulding process
that we aggregately term as the world,
life, or the universe.
And, some of us come to the valued

cognizance that high spiritual achievement
impart to us the special ability
of crystalizing the total, integrated mental vision
of all these imprints at will.
Thus, in whatever state of existence
things appear at a particular moment,
such a vision integrated will
embody the representation of all that has gone before.

The future and the past —
actions and reactions—are two aspects
of a state of the rational soul.
For example, if a plant in any season
is faced with severe deficiency
in its natural need of light and food,
definitely the resultant effects
are manifested in the form of many a wilting leaf
drying, and dying, stems and parts.
No matter what is done to make up
for the deficiency-induced fatality,
the damage remains
irreversible;
the mark of death is never quite erasable.
A deficiency in man's spiritual needs, by the way,
very much follows similar veins.
I am, therefore, inclined to believe
that a novel branch of medicine would evolve
to develop precise methods to treat, and deal
with, this type of problem and complication —
so that any serious malady
rooted in the past
is treated and cured,
uprooted fast!

***

Wholesale and sole researches in parapsychology,
bio-ecology and geneology,

likely indicate that probably heredity,
modulated with learnt traits and training,
is the basic sources of an individual's present state.

(As regard the body's role and the soul's goal
casting all past pretense and tense future tense,
little remains neigh.)
What is profusely evident,
however, is that the natural existence,
unknown to man,
goes from one unknown point to another —
the journey
of "I" to I.
This goes on without break or stoppage,
involuntarily, continually.
And, in this course, a human being is surely
also forming his imprints and image
in this unfolding scroll of mysterious existence —
all of his actions, thoughts and words,
intentions—existence of body and soul —
all inward and outward facets —
being imprinted on the infinite film of the nature,
moulding and being moulded by
the Existence
as a whole.

***

Spirit with matter —
The body, with the mind it contains —
in its current state, is like the center
of all, as a consequence
of all that was, is,
and is going to be!
Man's physical and spiritual life
is moulded in harmony
by the passing time, leading to his
present state, and reflected by the latter.

Laugh or weep —
as mentioned, this is like
an unfinished book of oneself,
a projection or manifestation on the screen
which leads to a condensation of form.
Definitely, how our mental and physical norm,
our existential aspect will relate
with the passage
of time,
will be cast deep
and will not easily be forgotten or erased.
Whenever the conditions lend favor,
the consequences will be manifested, will appear.
For, as has been true, from age to age,
as you sow, so you reap.

***

At that moment
of truth, we shall find
that all the events are alive
and true, reflecting ourselves,
and we see the reality—our reality —
in its totality:
which means that regardless of all
adverse conditions, we have achieved
a sort of resurrection, a certain enlightenment.

The causality to quote:
Our present condition will then be
like an indicator, a natural index,
being a result of all prior
incidents, accidents and occurrences.

When a sound signal—a whistle or a word —
leaves our mouth, it will carry its attributes,
its particular wavelength inclusive.
Its marked independence

over many stages and phases
during its propagation
in the atmosphere
from the origin to the destination
will generally be preserved intact.
Wherever there
is a susceptible, well oriented receiver,
the wave pattern can be captured
and regenerated precisely,
note by note.

Similarly, visual signals, images
can retain their intrinsic characteristics
precisely from the point of origin
to the point of destination—the screen;
and in a suitable projection,
the entire scene
can be serenely seen
in the same continuous manner
as the original has been,
with all the light-and-shadow pattern
and color and contrast
also reappearing through the film,
and expressly delivered through the light rays.

Sometimes these chareographics of shadow-and-light
may mask the reality, and deceive
us to think there is no correlation
between the source and the destination.
But these shadows and lights
but only replicate the original,
down to the level
of atoms, molecules, and waves,
reflecting truly how each entity
physically or metaphorically acts and behaves.

This, then is the uniform picture
of the eternal fate

in all our states of existence.
The ceaselessly propagating grand waves,
the ever moving prime pictures,
are always there
regardless of our perception and sensation
or awareness
of their presence.
One is able to perceive them a bit,
no doubt, with the help of one's senses;
but perhaps
man can witness
the play in its entirety,
see all of it,
far better
with his metaphysical faculty.
This law of nature,
which is the result of predestination,
is, needless to say, is equivalent
to the assumption of the free-will of the nature.
At this very moment,
our system, in a manner, has recorded everything
that we proudly own as our experience.
its unmistaken imprint is there —
in the wrinkled pages of our memory,
our electromagnetic body.
We are usually quite persistent
in denying this subtle underlying continuity,
mainly to bolster our precious ego;
and we tend to pretend
to try to know
ourselves—a perpetual quest of self-identity —
by denying our very own inherent
past and future,
fateful plight.

***

(What about worshipping, then, God Almighty?)
All told, all true religious messengers, emissaries, or masters,
in the area of ethics and morality
experienced and learned the genuine truth and wisdom
with the inner enlightenment
through the blissful vision
of the ultimate reality;
and as such always encouraged his disciples
to wholeheartedly and truthfully follow
the virtuous path of goodness,
while alerting their untamed minds
to the ultimate destination on the physical level
in the form of death.
This truth is not intangible,
but quite urgent,
to be known, with sincere hearts.
He travels that path
enduring many hardships, just to bring
this fateful message to his following
and to have them implement
its essence in the society.

Such a Messenger is a *God-send* mould.
The *God-minded* personality
of such a true learned one
merges into the absolute reality,
while his thoughts perpetually issue
truth from the laws of existence.
The complete balance and harmony
in their self-expression
come in the form of moulded words —
each word bearing its well chosen meaning.
Following their instructions is like being
placed behind a powerful microscope,
through which our own noble personality,
our own stronger character, higher happiness,
and the true meaning of prosperity and adversity

are explained.
Under the master's precept,
they become magnified
a millionfold.

***

Particles, like numbers, apparently seem discrete,
Confined in space, finite quantities, pretty petty entities.
In reality, however, if we meet
Their latent, potential form and feat,
We realize they extend unbound, limitlessly touching the
   infinities.

But in this world, we can find nothing that defies regulation
— Either in form or in substance, in meaning or in appearance —
That acts in dire contradiction
To the laws of Existence, under random fiction.
The rational element is ever present, in every turn and nuance!

So, particles within limited bound are finite; only elemental
Forms, with a negligible role as to the properties of the whole,
Or the absolute, or the monumental.
But they also possess a transcendental
Norm, where they're one with the universe, the infinite Soul.

***

If we examine the laws that exist
Describing the nature and its working,
Analysing what we see and what we do not,
We find how different the human body
Is from his true being: sublime consciousness.

Man's true essence, the very basic gist
Of his birth, life, action and being,
Is consciousness, presenting to him Camelot

Of relative comparisons, contrasts, images, melody:
Against limitations imposed by perceptions and senses.

***

The concept of good and evil, unity
And separation, reality and imagination,
Etcetera, have all come into being
Due to our limited sensual faculties.
Thus, our eye-sight is limited, but vision unlimited.

Our sensual perceptions, with limited agility
And form, determined by the specific function,
Construction and capabilities of the handicapped, erring
Faculties, create a veil over the realities;
To view the face of reality, that veil must be lifted.

Even in the constant aspects of an object,
We experience perpetual instability
Due to our senses' oscillations and vascillations
— This is an old knowledge, nothing new! —
The senses create a perturbing field of their own!

But if we look at the laws that direct
The magnetic field of the earth or its gravity,
Or the gravitational fields propagating through the constellations
Of trillions of galaxies, holding the orbits they drew
Of stars and planets that the Big Bang has flown,

Influencing all beings on every planet
Including our own, ourselves inclusive;
And if we endeavor to comprehend and to know
Our physical surrounding, and the nature's mystery,
Based merely on modulation of gross waves,

Then little would be the chance we'd unravel the secret
Of the nature, the ultimate truth would rarely give
Way to our enquiry and exploration—unless they go
To a point of perception and reception at the infinity,
Transcending the senses, unless the way true harmony paves.

Any imagination, hypothesis or elaboration
Our mind entertains, becomes limited, constrained
By space and time, by virtue of our senses
That receive the nature, acting as a physical instrument.
The sensory images are thus distorted, incomplete.

As if, the senses create an animation,
A cacoon, by which the reality becomes curtained;
An artificiality that surrounds, encircles, builds fences
Around, to hide the true knowledge inherent.
Subsequently, the image as real we begin to treat.

Thus we, led by our sensual perception, err badly;
The illusory elements, the false images cast
Long shadows on the true realities, and the real vision
Is lost and buried behind superficial covers.
Our personality remains helplessly bound,

Unable to grasp the real truth, sadly;
The real truth is perceptible only from the mast
Of the metaphysical realm, viewing the horizon
Meeting the infinity, that true knowledge ushers.
By brisk analyses of false images, the truth is never found.

Even a law, well-founded and well-checked,
May show imperfections as our knowledge subsequently grows.
Take, for example, Kepler's and Newton's laws
Of planetary motion, that's regarded long established,
And greatly respected in the domain of physics.

But the observation of a comet, whose twirling tail trekked
The sky at a speed of 550 km/sec., and whose nose
Lay at 52000 km from the sun, lo and behold! draws
Circumstantial evidence to make these laws look blemished,
Fallible like child's toys, and the truth yet to fix.

Any object will have its specific gravity
About twice as much on the planet earth
As on the Jupiter, and only half as much
On the Venus; and on the Eros, its weight
Would be smaller yet, due to the Eros's diameter nominal.

This inevitably makes us aware of relativity -
A principle that the learned know gave birth
To the concept of time as the fourth dimension, such
That the limitations regarding it are taken as innate;
And the entire new philosophy of time appears whimsical.

It is thus derived from celebrated experiments
That time is to be based on the finite, constant speed of light.
If this premise be dropped, and if instead we adopt
Light's velocity as infinite, or varying with the reference
Frame, many natural phenomena would appear quite absurd.

Relativity rules physical theories to the greatest extent:
Cause and effect, motion and the state of rest or flight,
Potential and kinetic energy—no matter what we opt
To consider, relativistic comparisons govern each occurrence;
And our perception must develop an apt logic for the events
    observed.

But, then, if an object could be completely isolated
And observed in its own domain, without relativistic
Effects, many of the familiar laws may falter,
Appearing contradictory and untenable and inaccurate;
For, then common attributes and definitions fall apart —

As, in isolation, each object's standard is slated
By itself; and in that sense, any law we pick,
Even though normally "fixed", would become thereafter
Subject to reassessment; so the ultimate fate
Of a law is intimately tied to the assumptions at the start.

Thus distinction between a uniform square
And a triangle, a circular motion and a linear one —
And all sorts of details, a total general scrutiny —
Are essential to establish laws, universal or specific.
(A neglect of these would only lead to lawlessness!)

For example, take an èlectron in an electric wire,
Undergoing a uniform linear motion,
Or a gas confined in a given space tiny —
They all have their laws, general or specific;
But, with changed conditions, any law's validity is void or under
    stress.

Again, for example, consider the periodic motion
Occurring every 24 hours: each moment itself
Of this period has a completely different place,
A different measure, a different significance,
When viewed from another frame of reference in the universe.

So, while a particular law has obviously done
Its job of governing the motion, it'll hardly help
To get the varying period for a new relativistic case.
The disorderly-looking motion of gaseous particles, for
    instance,
Are really orderly paths under specific laws terse.

To explain this paradox, one more example follows.
Suppose you have a yarn, say, 50 meters long,
And you want to make a spherical ball out of it.
For this, the spacing between the fingers you employ
To wind the thread is clearly quite important

As a critical dynamic parameter, to which the yarn then owes
The specific or peculiar shape to which it'll belong.
Now, devising a law for this case may probably confound the
    wit,
But the inherent motion of the thread might quite likely enjoy
Orderly laws, the type to which a spherical gas mass is pursuant.

So, even seemingly random motions are inherently
Orderly, otherwise the orderly outcomes would be missing
— This explanation by Sir James Haines also brings to mind
The theory about the motion and lifetime of the stars,
Which with the laws of gases bears a great deal of resemblance.

With the existing instrumentation, we cannot follow
    permanently
The paths of the gaseous particles, from the very beginning
To the end, and therefore we disregard the disorder behind
That motion, and see beyond the apparent chaos that somewhat
    bars
A clear view of the ordered gaseous behavior pattern, for
    instance.

***

Our tendency to generally seek order, however,
Is prompted by the observation that the nature, by and large,
Exhibits inherent order—all things, indeed, seem to be subject
To some grand order, and nothing is really without it.
Thus order, in some form or degree, reigns in the universe.

So, if we should consider a beginning for Creation and thereby
    endeavor
To observe the minutest order of motion of particles and charge -
Assemblies, then the question of gas masses' order perfect
Within the apparent disorder would attain a final fit
Answer (for instance, the atomic structure might the mystery
    disperse!)

In any case, the seemingly irregular movements involved
Do ultimately generate an overall orderly pattern.
If we view these phenomena with the eye of knowledge
And wisdom, they would open the door of the truth sooner.
When I view a blossom at beauty's zenith, it captures my soul.

What's the source of beauty and order dissolved
In its stems, petals and roots that, penetrating deep in the soil,
   earn
The essence of life for it, with so much artfulness on the stage
Of nature, with precision—as if, in dirt, Existence's heart we
   discover,
The manifestation of the highest order grown from a muddy
   hole.

A painter with his palette and brush tries to paint its beauty,
Trying to capture the subtle order, detached from everything
   else.
He picks up the brush to put on the canvas
The most delicate aspect conceived in his mind
Imparting a new life to its stems and petals.

The painter's brush moves, then stops, then moves again, with
   duty
And ecstasy, trying to create; while the nature's brush sure
   dwells
In the saga of continuous creation, from the leptonic to the
   galactic mass,
Never stopping or flopping; each spectacle, each speck well
   defined.
The more we see and find, the deeper our admiration settles.

Could one have comprehended that such fresh, delicate petals,
Such zeniths of beauty, could spring from a hard stem,
Or dark wood, or an unseeming, ungainly source?

What really makes the flower bloom, and dance, excel?
Who imparted these wonderous qualities and abilities to it?

If it's the atmospheric pressure that gently lulls
The petals to fold at eventide, and the rays at sunrise wake them
Up, even then there has to be a paramount principle, a fateful
  force,
That enables the bud to grow, and to assume this color and
  smell;
That enabled the environment to act as its attributes' marvellous
  conduit.

It's because of that force that the nature deemed it to come
Out of that shell and veil in this particular shape,
And color and scent, etcetera, in such a substained manner!
I can smell its fragrance scattered in the air all around,
Penetrating each pore of the space with sweetness uniquely
  its own.

As if, it were a newborn, pretty nymph—beauty's plenum,
Sweetly proud of its charms, conscious that no one'll escape
From noticing its coming in flying colors; and the tall flying
  banner
Of its fragrance should reach each point, and even the eternity
  astound;
And would touch and be lost in the infinity's supreme
  subliminal zone.

It's incessantly moving toward that goal intense.
From where has it got the urge to be one with the infinity?
And what exactly is the relationship between the eternity and it?
Where is the source of force that empowers and guides it?...
  This all
— Which man's mind is so incapable of comprehending?

It is evident that it is the Universal Mind, the Will of Existence,
Or whatever other name be given to it, with dignity and
   integrity.
Everything is being guided by it—from the speck in the pit
To the grandest galaxy of stars—and everything is following
   a call
To be moving toward the eternity, Existence's Will thoroughly
   attending.

And, what's superbly interesting is that, from the plants to
   animals and man
All beings are moving toward the eternity incessantly.
All are possessed and preoccupied, completely absorbed,
   enslaved
By this superlative force, each being to its own destiny.
It's a procession that includes whatever it is that exists.

Isn't the earth itself, with revolutionary motions that scan
The skies, as it were, suspended in the space, searching gallantly
The clue to some premordial mystery, not all-too-well behaved;
And going round and round in a state of bewilderment, in
   a mini-
Madness day and night, dashing to points its destiny enlists?

Who is exerting on it the pull of gravitational attraction,
And the contrifugal force, to maintain the balance?
Where are the interim stations, and the ultimate destination?
— The caravan of Existence journeys yonder ceaselessly —
With the galaxies, stars, planets, creatures, minerals—all
   aboard.

All are unquestionably guided by an absolute determination,
Obeying unconditionally a Superconsciousness, true
   uncommonsense —
An uncompromising supreme command driving everything, by
   ration,

In accordance with its own nature and capacity, to its destiny.
And where's the Commander, and what's He got in His mind
    stored?

Can He be here and not there? How can He be not everywhere —
From the limits of the galaxies, to the bottom of the ocean?
Is He other than Existence, or is Existence other than Him?
Or is He in Existence (— for all are reflection of Him, though
Anything is not quite Him, as an image is not the mirror.)

Therefore, Existence is the oneness of all, the singularity in
    every layer
Enshrined. Neither you nor me or anything else is other than
    that One—
Unfolding of this scroll of the universe! Other? Absolute
    presence other than Him
I know not—All I know is that, whoever did not tend to go
To "other", cognized the truth of Existence—a cognition that's
    sure to occur.

***

This, then, is the cognition of the truth of Existence.
Spinoza says: the mind and the body in reality are not apart;
But they are two different manifestation of the essence —
The existence of God: "He is both body and essence, soul and
    heart:

    Since He is with all of them, supreme;
      Indeed, there is no other than Him."

***

The greater man's awakening,
The greater his knowledge of Existence;
The greater opening of his inner eyes and vision,
The more acute his own awareness of his being
Full of ignorance—to gain knowledge's essence,
The above is the wise's first step, the firmest decision!

***

The most learned man is he
Whose personality is in harmony
With the truth and the essence
Of the nature, of the Existence,

Even though the relationship of his character
And his personality with the truth of the nature
May seem miraculous to us,
Hardly anything exists in the universe

That cannot be found in man's
Inner-self, his inner universe, sans
His boundless greed and desire,
That dig his grave, light his funeral pyre!

His unrestrained attachments
Chain him down below, keeping him from the saint's
High and exalted position; his dependencies
On redundant objects and sensual tendencies

Degrade and corrupt him absolutely.
If man were to erase resolutely

All images, to just see God, he would
Reach His rank with his spirit renewed!

Man in his own truth can bring
About the perception of everything
Found in the universe, subject
To the use of specimen perfect

Or model or virtual representation.
What causes man's eminent position
To be degraded is his dependence
And reliance on his perceptions, on sense -

Organs that distort them in proportion
Of their limited capabilities (and shun
The ultimate reality, that veils
Of ignorance cover, that prevails!)

If the self of man was to refine,
He would be elevated to the divine
Utmost spiritual state he treasures,
Surpassing all fatal ill-measures

And causes and handicaps that bind.
The state of Man he'd then find.
He, in this state, is the meaning
Of God's name, true worship and thanksgiving.

Then, and therefore, his identity
Is honored with the Viceregency
Of God in nature; in Existence
He is the manifestation of God's essence.

Abol Abbas Amoli, the Sufi great
Of his time, once chanced to have met
Someone who desired a story of a special
Miracle, or a blessing for the day especial;

And answered Amoli, "What can be more
Miraculous than the fact that, as a daily chore
For my living, I slaughtered sheep before;
But, thank God! I'm not doing that any more.

Now I'm living God's own blessing.
God opened the door of knowledge, the spring
Of His fervor to me.—This knowledge was the key supreme,
To fetch saints like Abu Said Abel-Kheyr to beseech me."

The wisdom that Abol Abbas is hinting
At, is not the type that follows by printing,
Or pouring over scholarly books, or practices similar.
Rather, it's the inner harmony mentioned earlier.

In closing his eyes to all outward
Attractions, with his inner vision well prepared
To receive his soul's singular signal —
He found his true self, at the summit of metaphysical

And spiritual ascent that one could bring
To bear; his wisdom was through meaning
And not through make-belief appearance:
— Such are saints' traits we see in Abbas's stance!

The means of truly wise to think
Are simple, and yet difficult—a mysterious link
Between the divine vision and ordinary human blind!
The sensitivity of the enlightened mind

Can perhaps be contrasted with a person's feelings
Who painstakingly scrutinizes just superficial things!
An enlightened mind, in contrast, observes
And identifies only with the essence of the universe!

But the observer of the superficial and the temporary
Perishes with the fleeting object; on the contrary,

True wisdom's view from the angles profound
Has always sought the deeper meaning, and verily found.

In accordance with their individual capacity,
In balanced and designated proportionality,
Men and women have received qualitites, attributes
From the nature; but their sum-total, from the top to the roots

Of knowledge and capability—vision of the eyes
Inner—has been offered by the nature to the wise!
Haven't we seen some of them who are
A home of compassion and courage, by far

The greatest there is to be seen among men?
If they see someone distressed or oppressed, they then
Feel for the weak or the sufferer of bars, infliction,
Denial of opportunity to progress, or interdiction,

With overflow of love and care-filled heart,
As might a loving mother for her child off-guard.
But while carrying their mission—God's will and command —
Their true tenacity and courage stand as a brand!

***

Such a unique synthesis, point of balance
Belongs to the truly perfect ones who thence
Can guide others to perfection pointedly,
With inner and outer strength, capabilities medley.

Because of their great mental faculty,
And deep awareness, and potent multi-
Dimensional precise powers, delicate and strong,
They symbolize the triumph of the right over wrong!

They offer guidance to the humanity as such,
Like lighthouses guiding ships off harm's touch.

Their words are lessons to be learnt and followed;
They build with life—let's walk that road!

***

I've come across people, I'm sad to say,
Who claim to be scholars, pathfinders of the day;
Educators of mankind they certainly claim to be,
But they are so naive and unbelievably clumsy,

That their greatest achievement is to pass judgment
On the works of great people; their thinking inherent,
Their mental bent and imagination self-indulgent,
And life's twisted image—are all always spent

But to lure them far off, away from their goal.
So, years of struggle only makes them broken-soul.
They wind up their search, really, only empty-handed;
Having little to offer, their words're heavy, dead,

Their sentences empty attempting to fill long discourses.
With no spirit to cognize the truth, the nature's forces
They ceremoniously pretend to pursue and adore;
They fight logic, pitting their ignorance-store.

I remember an episode of some years ago,
When I was invited to a cultural show
Consisting of music, dance, play, part-by-part,
And organized by an old friend, a lover of art.

For some reason still beyond my reach,
The person supposed to deliver the opening speech
Did not show up at all, just sent his apology —
This made my friend quite nervous and desperately turn
to me.

He knew my ability in speaking, and entreated
Me to come to his rescue, and I gracefully accepted.

75

I called my selfishness, with self-grandiosement my bout —
A favor to my friend, an act of helping out!

My friend then went off with a happy, beaming face,
On being assured that I'd see him through the distress.
And I used all my assets and ability with language
To make the strange address through a maze of pompous
phrases!

The blessed topic now I don't even recall!
But under the circumstances, I wasn't bad at all!
I did my best, with my youthful mind and zeal;
Ventured in front of the gathering, and the show I did steal!

Thousands of intent eyes were staring at me straight;
And I took a moment to let my nerves compensate
For the suddenness of the ordeal, and numbness in my feet —
Let alone in my mind—for which it was no minor feat.

At any rate, the task was fulfilled in a manner!
My mind quickly darted and delivered whatever matter
It could urgently muster—which hardly had any value,
Scholarship, or much substance, for that matter, I tell you!

However, the people were ecstatic, so impressed!
As if they had some great discovery just witnessed;
Or, as if, I had resolved life's prime issues —
Such warm response did even me completely confuse —

As I myself felt like having done the same —
(Namely, made a great discovery, or a wild issue tame)!
Now, luckily, I generally prefer to get rid of my ignorance
And, hence, don't pride myself on such an episode or chance.

As for my audience, they probably complimented
Me out of plain courtesy and etiquette well-intended:
For, such a bewildered piece of work my speech extempore —
A hatched collection of ideas patched-up on the floor —

Must have been, with parts borrowed from my predecessors
And thinkers and ancestors, psychology and music professors:
That little did it contain substance of mine own!
Then, what was it I was doing?—This event'd surely shown

    That I adventured to render a long rambling speech
    Most enthusiastically, to an audience clearly each
    Of whom was inert, inattentive, or lay.
    I just wanted to pass the time, save face, and the day.

Or, it might not have been completely improbable
That I endeavored to demonstrate how capable,
And knowledgeable, and mentally agile, and wise
I was to size the occasion, and to it conspicuously rise. . . .

***

    My point in making such an elaboration
    Is to comment on the gift of gab, on oration,
    That is practiced by many of the speakers;
    Indeed, my act was not unlike that of most leaders.

In general, I've listened with utmost care
To speeches of others of name and fame rare,
And often found them portraying only airy pictures,
As I did in the episode above, with few strictures.

For intance, if a speaker by a podium proudly stands,
And only recounts his transport over air, water, lands
With great solemnity or gaiety, I do not quite know
What exactly gives him the happiness, pride and ego

    About the whole business—an a-priori preoccupation
    He bears himself mentally, or the apparent admiration
    Reflected in the looks and the rapt attention, silence
    He receives on his speech from the clumsy audience.

The wise always refrain from long drawn-out speech;
From being overly zealous over trifles; from a breach
Of people's trust, confidence; from abusing in any way
The freedom given them as to action, thought, and say.

They seldom utter a word till they know it to be the truth,
And only in a manner so that people can see the truth;
His aim is not to act or to make the audience gasp —
His saying has solid basis the listeners can easily grasp.

To criticize speakers or audience is not my intention;
But merely to convey a thought I thought it fit to mention —
That whenever we appear somewhere to make a presentation,
We must know and realize the truth, our real station,

Our view-point and pertinent facts, phrases, mode;
so, others spending time and trust become not snowed,
Misled, betrayed, mistreated, neglected or simply slanted.
The audience should never....never be taken for granted

To continue to take any worthless word or gab.
They should surely benefit, as they pick up the tab
On time, attention, trust — their investment is no less.
(...And I hope the reader shares the view of this address!)

***

To explain, once again,
the reason main
I've gone in such details regarding speakers
And audience, is because
the speakers arouse
Such sensitive vibrations — be it boon or curse!

The speaker at the podium
sees as pendulum
The audience's heads swinging, swaying as the sea —

Offering eager agreement
to his words ardent,
And showing vehemently it is his own cup of tea!

But, thinking without bias,
isn't it obvious
That the significance of this mutual play
Is that these're simple
signs that do dribble
The sure sense of selfishness and egotism lay?

Though the sayings are
Such to go very far
Rarely; nor is there any scientific value in these.
With no intellectual content,
or any spiritual bent,
The words are shallow symbols of both the parties.

Presenting a scientific
truth or a topic
For the purpose of enlightenment of the public —
Mind is significant,
and its value surely can't
Be discounted—I must of course be quick

To point the self-evident
Fact; my sole intent
Centers on the common exchange people employ
On collective fora, or,
Alas! often even for
Personal touch, which goes a-begging truth or joy!

***

Hegel said, "Everything is present
In the conscious public mind—under falsity and truth!
However, it takes a great man, a true saint
To search for, and find, the grand truth.

Whoever can know what the need is
Of the world, of his time, in his own real time,
And can offer it through teaching, also following his
Own precept himself, makes his word sublime.''

Therefore, to seek prestige as an intellectual
And scholar through sheer eloquence
And beautiful words and speeches, without any actual
Benefit to others is blasphemy, nonsense,

And pretty selfish act, a self-serving tact
On part of the speaker of the type
Referred above; it's shameful, as a matter of fact,
A black spot on character, quite difficult to wipe.

When I met a person (a not-too-uncommon event!),
Who happened to be known as a scholar
Great—I must confess, to my great disappointment,
That 'fore he knew me, or the matter,

Or how much value his words might have
For me, or being even questioned,
He started to speak, not waiting to save
A word to find if I mentioned

What it was that I really needed;
But spoke as if his sole
Role intended was to display how learned
He was—a pretty dubious goal!

St. Augustine has said that the truth remains
Hidden from man's eyes, because he
Becomes a slave—bound helplessly in chains —
Of what he was supposed to be

A master of—a sad irony of role-reversal!
Socrates, in his speech for defense

In his trial, said, "Chearephon goes to the temple
Of Delphi one day, to seek guidance,

And asked Apollo, the sun god, if there'd been
Any one more learned than Socrates.
And a voice answered—(though no one was seen) —
'There was none more learned than Socrates!'

When I heard about the anonymous voice,
I wanted to know the real, full meaning
Behind it all: as I knew of course
I knew not much, almost nothing!

But I thought doubtlessly I knew indeed
That God, for one, would never lie.
So, I wanted to know what I was to read
In God's words heard from up in the sky!

For a long...long time I pondered on the event;
Then I started to test myself. Well,
After meeting many a scholar, and saint"
Socrates on the story continued to dwell —

"After much travel and search, rather odd
As it may seem, I finally found
That, as the only one who knows truly all is God,
The Providence's God-send sound —

Was just meant to show that what knowledge
Any man whosoever owns is so
Very insignificant! For, if He truly says
My name for a person who happens to know,

Supposedly, the most in this world—that means
That even the most knowledgeable person,
Socrates, still knows very little—(so, one gleans
Mere pebbles on the endless shores of the ocean)!"

The wisdom of Socrates' story truly transcends time.
My master, in his sublime teaching also said,
"Knowledge is a receptive ear, to catch each rhyme,
And not a verbal tongue to lash out instead!"

Ultimately, one must really observe the dictum —
That the truth is that a wise teacher
Does a good student in spirit become,
Enamoured by the beauty and goodness of the nature.

If Mankind didn't spoil himself with childish selfishness,
But rather harmonized with the truth, the nature,
Then man's capability might well spell success,
Like the powerful crane that lifts far greater

Loads than the force the operator may apply.
Thus, great mental and spiritual feats and wonder
May be realized as the source of energy-supply
Gets well developed, and properly directed under

The intellect truly sublimated, the spirit fully lifted,
And the precious spiritual jewels duly gifted.
Herbert Spencer said, "In every act committed,
It is far better to see the meaning that fitted

The event, the object's nature, the nature's objects,
Than to learn just the meaning of words —
Be it for mental, moral or spiritual prospects
Or for training. Indeed it is far better for us

To contemplate on what naturally occurs
All around us, than to procure the benefits
Of different languages and cultures,
And to master their distinctions like the Pundits!

For, the soul's full acquaintance and harmony
With the truth of nature, is the knowledge true!
Beyond the sensory perceptions, emotions—ecstasy, agony —
One touches the nature, sees the knowledge true.

Having reached this point of harmony with the truth of nature,
Having attained thus full self-awareness,
Man truly masters the inherent knowledge mature,
And intimate root-connections he establishes.

***

Humility reigning high, he may perceive or say
That he knows almost next to nothing.
But, let knowledge be filtered, and distilled—if it may
Be purified this way, in order to bring

    About the purest concentrate—then such a man indeed
    Possesses such a potent and pure drop of nectar!
    As Kant said, "Someone or something can not breed,
    Just by virtue of being beautiful, or open a new world afar!

But the perception of beauty is a beautiful thing —
A realization of this requires an invocation
Of a special quality, of a true greatness harboring,
And sparks up a new spirit, a novel inspiration.

    It's not their outer attributes that make them beautiful
    In our eyes, as those qualities are yet in veils;
    Rather, it's a power in them with a powerful pull
    That our spirit and consiousness completely compels.

Invoking resonant powers resident in our soul,
It stimulates every atom of our entire being.
This resonance, identity and harmony play the role
Of inducing reverberations with the songs the angels sing!

    We do not perceive the music
    Of any object, but the powerful note
    We hear is but the intrinsic
    Note our own soul wrote!"

***

83

Death is an evolutionary step, indeed,
Toward lifting the dark veils drawn upon
The infinite absolute!
But life and death serve the same creed —
This paramount truth upon us must dawn.
For, who can refute
That life and death are reflections that feed
The vision from the mirror of the universal pantheon,
The Existence's stages by statute!

* 1 *

Life and death are the precisely changing images
Of the Existence, for the purpose of fulfilling a pledge
Ordained, a mission determined, for every age,
By Existence, for our being's various phases.
  According to the physical and metaphysical scientists,
  The after-effects of the physiological and anatomical
  Changes persist beyond death, like shadows subtle
  Lingering past the horizon. The soul in this world exists
As the prime element, motivating the evolution of these
  For reaching their perfection, undergoing transformations
    Without perishing, like simply wearing different garments,
In accordance with time, place, circumstances, personalities,
  In order to facilitate the evolution and liberation, once
    For all, of the inner being, from this world's events.

* 2 *

Before coming to this point in the space-time continuum,
It has gone through the steps of the evolutionary ladder;

And it is wearing the present attire—the fabrics Existence could
  gather —
as a continuation of the same process, the fulcrum
  Of this lively lever being the soul's liberation!
  After death too, in order to adapt to extant environment,
  It must undo all the previous efforts spent,
  And embark on a new vehicle for the sake of continuation
Of the journey of the full liberation of the inner being.
  Descartes said: Any change in this world has a role
    In, and is an intimate part of, the totality of things.
Leibniz, in his book "On the Principles of Nature", does bring
  Out the interesting concept that birth tends to keep the goal
    Of permitting chance to study it, of Time to ride its wings:

* 3 *

"In the gradual natural progression of life may this goal bask!
However, death seems to reverse this process very quickly,
Making a comprehension of this progression rather unlikely —
A proper vision of this inherent evolution a tantalizing task!"
  If there was a certain discontinuity in the changes
    From life to death, all evolutionary processes in every form
    Ranging from primitive algae, cylindrical bacteria, myriad
      worm
    Species, mysterious traces and fossil remains from the bygone
      days
Of extinct creatures, the very puzzling riddle of death and
  Life would have become transparent, less baffling at any rate.
    The process of evolution and self-reproduction of the green
      algae,
And their branching out into multiple subspecies present
  a grand
    Caravan of life, a milestone of existence—though its fate
      Still wears a mask of mystery, an insoluble riddle rides its
        story.

However, this doctrine—that everything is evolving,
Being guided toward its own destination most precisely —
Is so fine that no scientific observation can surmise the
Key to it, or detect or observe evidences for solving
   This riddle—a shortcoming that makes scientists perplexed;
   So that, in ignorance and confusion, many measures and
      standards
   And mouldings are employed for reference to birds
   Animals, humans, plants, etc.; yet the mystery stays
      unflexed.
Nevertheless, definitely, what cannot be denied
   Is that the evolving being is continually progressing through
   The alternate steps of life and death ... and life again!
This law in fact does predominantly provide
   The determination of the map or route true
      Of Existence, which designed life and death, neither in
      vain!

Transformation as a step to evolution is the hallmark
Of the nature's endless facets—see the snake's moulding each
   year,
For instance, the significance of which is hard to measure;
Or, consider a container of water over the stove—the arc
   Of the flame would make the water's temperature rise:
   Initially slowly, and then rapidly, as the water begins to boil.
   For an observer, it may take great effort and toil
   To measure fully all changes of state at each phase and guise
Of the water, even though, on the whole, it may
   Generally be only a rather short interval of time
      For the whole set of transformations to have taken place.
The same applies, of course, to every occurrence everyday!
   Of the endless comings and goings, without reason or rhyme,
      Or gradual progression, nothing comes or goes in any case!

At times, however, it may sort of just so happen
That something appears to us to go or to happen
Suddenly, as if accidently, without adequate explanation
Or gradual progression, or systematic repetition now and then!
    Waiting or searching for the comforting appearance
    Of step-by-step explanation, or detailed manifestation
    Is like serving the inherent subtle mutual interrelation
    That everything has by the nature's scheme (and not by only
        chance).
Disbelieving in this type of relationship
    Is like disconnecting the line between cause
        And effect and the internal harmony involved.
But, in the last analysis, as the ultimate tip,
    It may be stated that the fine line between cause
        And effect may be nil, in a chain of continuity dissolved.

More precisely, cause and effect barely bear true contiguity
In time, nor a homogeneous spatial balance or correspondence.
Indeed, the four-fold dimensionality of space and time and,
    hence,
Their complex interrelations lead to the common obscurity

(Of the inevitable causal interactions among happenings;
Of the intrinsic non-vanishing projections of points,
Lines, planes, solid figures, events, connections, joints;
Of reasons, seasonal transitions: the spring to the fall; falls, seas
    from springs;)
    Of the basic relationship between cause and effect —
        Even though we carry their legacy every instant,
        And they are bound to us to nurture our future!
    It is, as if, the effect, as a foetus select,
        Having developed for a period as the womb's occupant
        In the cause, the mother, must be born, as a law of nature!

The soul has been the subject of much research throughout
The ages; inquisition and enquiries into its nature
Have continued ceaselessly, but the stature
Of its definition remains illusive, clouded with doubt.
    And yet the simplest definition that one could
    Give of the soul is that it's free of any attribute
    Or association, even though, without an alibi or substitute,
    It plays the true role of man, his character, aptitude,
All through one's lifetime; and even though we see,
    Looking through different lenses, called at times,
    By different observers as science, or human frailty,
Or human knowledge, or learning of the key
    Of the secret of life, etcetera; and sing the hymns
        Of the soul by these attributes—but of all these, it's free!

None of these attributes is the soul's creator!
So the absence of any of these attributes
Doesn't imply the soul's non-existence, nor puts
An end to its existence; the soul's existence is greater,
    And intrinsicly transcendental. The soul is independent
    Of all attributes, characteristics, constraints, matter.
    As Mark Aurel has said: "The stars' gift'll be reclaimed;
        Whatever
    Comes from ashes will return to ashes, the ascent
Or descent of dust to dust, water to water,
    Fire to fire, ether to ether, and air to air,
        Layer by layer, share by share, element by element,
Is inevitable; and yet the nature
    Of desire is such that each wish will ensnare
        And hold one captive save one's divine birth, final ascent!"

Buddha said, "After my new birth, death ceases;"
Death perishes following this new birth, final ascent!
Each state we pass in life yields basis for development
Of a different self-identity; and if our desire decreases
   To the extent that we become fully detached and free
   From our own attributes, regardless of their specific
   Character or pattern, then and then only we pick -
   Up the ultimate knowledge of the nature of death—the sea
Of non-being, as it were, a total and absolute naught!
   A final severance, separation, a departure without return!
      Yet death as isthmus is just an apparent form; truly there's
An inner continuity in life and death. In the Nature's thought
   Harmony prevails, and continuity is characteristic of its
pattern;
      As the spectrum is continuous, but separate colors one
      sees.

With regard to life and death, too, similarly,
These're viewed as different states—being and non-being;
We normally view life as opposite to death; a pure keying
To knowledge will reveal, however, that quite superbly
   Life and death are borne of each other; without separation
   Or boundary; they are continuous states, indeed,
   Of existence. The duality and oneness existing in the seed
   And the tree, the drop and the ocean, matter and animation,
Are, in essence, the nature's manifestations intimate!
The unity underlying all diverse forms of manifestation
Is the fundamental law of Existence we have to bring -
   Out to reside in our consciousness, which could open the gate
      Of true cognizance of the secret of existence, of attestation —
      That there is continuity invariably present in everything!

Hegel has said, "We human beings are
Just temporary, different manifestations
Of the eternal, vital essence (that runs
Through life and death freely, from the farthest star
   To the speck of dust under our very own feet)!
   We are, as it were, the miniature reproduction
   Of boundless potentialities of the nature's evolution!
   But if we should compare these, the implicit
Void of endless spatial and temporal discontinuity,
   (And between the sublime potentiality and the stark reality)
     May become apparent and man should see
His nothingness (because of his self-induced frailty,
   And failure to attain his intended height, divine quality)
     Which is man's true misfortune, and a profound pity!"

Materialists have not and will not recognize
What the principle of existential originality says
Through the current and assimilated natural changes.
In fact, a correct way to surmise a quiz of this size,
   To investigate such a difficult problem the trick,
   Is just not to accept things of which our senses
   Have not a definite or complete knowledge.
   It's not right to placate our minds with trivial logic.
The discussion I recently had with a friend
   Of mine may throw some light on this topic —
     On the materialistic point of view of the nature,
On the eternal nature of the soul—(that end -
   -Less source of controversy and view myopic,
     And of perplexity, anxiety, illusion, caricature!)

* 14 *

I said that nothing in this world can be
Totally annihilated, as matter must obey
The principle of conservation (which means that it may
Change from one form into another, including energy;
    But it cannot undergo destruction into, or creation
    From, absolutely nothing); and, besides, you see,
    Existence isn't confined to matter—look at you and me!
    My friend, however, kept insisting that none
Of my arguments mattered, for matter was all
    There was, and nothing but matter mattered, existed
        In the universe, and matter was devoid of conscience
Or consciousness, or thought, or intelligence—call
    It whatever one might; so, then, one was just led
        To conclude that the universe had no intelligence!

* 15 *

He thus wanted to convince me, win me through.
I, for one, do not intend to argue as—for or against —
Prejudiced people, nor do I have any taboo against
Receiving good thoughts and alternative points of view.
    But I'm generally not given to the idea of
    Blindly accepting anything. If you do not
    Have the proper perspective, the rational thought,
    Then you might fail to put a full-stop
To the error I'm committing. With that type of attitude,
    On the other hand, you couldn't share
        My gained knowledge, the discoveries I've made.
So, it's best it is fully understood
    That for the recognition of the truth, stern or fair,
        Observation, experience and attitude do offer great aid.

I've to put the physical aspects of man
Under a microscope and endeavor to explain
To him how these physical aspects normally gain
Their very forms and functions by virtues greater than
    Plain material in nature. Even in the brain cells,
    Whose life expectancy is longer than any other
    Type of cell (so that many regard them further
    On gaining an eternal life than anything else),
As in everything else, there are constant changes
    From one form to another. I've to usher his attention
      To let him witness how everything in the human body
Is constantly changing, with varying rates and ranges!
    How could something that is constantly on the run,
      Be the absolute essence, the symbol of stability?

The organisms suffering numberless changes can't
Very well be the source or the ultimate cause
Of the body, much less of the absolute self. Pause
Then we must, to ask the question: What is constant
    After all? What's the reason for this strange lack
    Of knowledge about our real, absolute, inner self?
    The answer is: It's because we constantly delve
    Into matter, even when seeking the spirit; blindly back
The body when intending to salvage the soul!
    The essence has been badly tied with the superficial.
      We, consequently, come to know only the body, the tools
And remain ignorant of the soul, missing our goal.
    We then end up regarding physical observation, the sensual
      Perception as the ultimate knowledge, acting like fools!

To support this view the materialist philosophers use
A hypothesis in physics; which states: "The internal
Energy of an isolated body becomes equal
To zero." This pew the materialist philosophers use
    To prove their point; to call the world as a composite
      of action -
    Reaction packages, mechanical and automatic, for example.
    Now, in my earlier book, "Chanteh", I've included ample
    Thoughts on how the existence of the effect tracks none
But the implicit cause; the created does simply manifest
    The creator, as a reliable, precise indicator, index.
      It follows as a corollary, then, that the creator's presence
In the created is necessary, imperative, and inevitable; lest
    The created should cease to exist if the creator exits, takes
      Leave, withdrawing the vested power, the spirit's essence!

In short, the object of creation is the first proof,
The grossest manifestation, of the creator's creative power.
Separation of the creative thought from the created would
    devour
And destroy the object's very existence—as of the pillars from
    a roof!
    Now, let's look at the example of a watch from this
    Perspective, and assume a point in time when, for instance,
    Watches didn't exist (didn't have a physical appearance).
    Imagine also a thinker intent on inventing one, who spent his
Time observing the planetary movements, pondering each day
    On a suitable method of measuring time, moment by
      moment;
      Visualizing, as a first step, what his objective might be.
Next, he uses appropriate instruments to perform an array
    Of measurements as conceived, till his hours well spent
      Bear fruit, and his conception of a watch becomes a reality.

The important points to bear in mind for us:
The inventor's inherent knowledge is the invariable prime here;
   indeed,
That knowledge is more important than the very watch, its need
Paramount is self-evident; for, the full-fledged watch *minus*
   That knowledge will leave us no watch. The very object
   Simply becomes extinct without the knowledge behind it.
   The parts and body of the watch are merely pieces, a bit
   Under the inventor's control, and embody the direct
Implementation of his knowledge-base (engineering and design -
   Concept, artificial intelligence's 'expert system', so to say!).
     Moreover, the knowledge of watch-making doubtlessly
      does depend
On the inventor, the predecessor—though a benign
   Neglect to this facet tend to bear we often may
     Due to certain reasons; such as, existence's continuous
      trend!

The inventor is the center of the evolutionary spectrum;
All the changes that occur to the material parts
And elements of the watch to gear motion that charts
The passage of time are considered as the outcome
   Of the inventor's knowledge; so the creator certainly is
   The most crucial element of the creation—the watch; its ways
   And design-details are the product of his knowledge.
   And surely the inventor'd just the thought prior to the
     practice.
Similarly, a carpenter may have all the knowledge
   of carpentry, but not having the tools requisite,
     He might not implement it, which of course doesn't mean
He doesn't have the knowledge—these examples raise
   The analogy of the nature of the soul, and the relationship it
     Bears with the body: The soul doesn't consist of matter,
      nor on it lean!

The body is the corporeal aspect of existence,
(Existence's implementation in material terms,
Pretty gross matter the body is—carrying the germs
Of diseases, old age, death, birth; and, hence,
   Analogous to the invention, the creation. The creator
   Or, rather, the creator's knowledge, is analogous
   To the soul, the spirit, that gives real life to us;
   That exists perennially, earlier than birth and later
Than death; that is pure inner being, absolute
   Existence, the crucial element, the supreme source,
      From which all material elements of life emanate;
Not within sight or mental grasp, but the body's seed and root;
   Eternal, indestructible; changing body in the course
      Of life after death, as one changes garments, date by date!)

My friend, whose opinion is based on the study
Of material philosophy, is saying what the English
Scholar and philosopher, John Stuart Mills did also publish —
"The core of the self—one's personality —
   Is derived from impressions and memories.
   Whatever enters the mind and is in the memory retained
   For future manifestation, follows the set trend
   Of continual updating for recurring use, as one thinks and
      sees
Fit, according to its composition and format etcetera.
   From a collective perception and presentation of all these,
      One derives the concept of 'I', and calls it one's
         personality.
The understanding of an object outside the era
   Of our inner frame, external to our inner boundaries,
      Is, by association and sensual perception, developing its
         identity."

* 24 *

Analyses of even these types of opinions of scholars
Lead to the conclusion that, at no point in life,
One remains stationary. For, each moment, in momentous
    triumph,
Gives birth to a train of ideas, sensual experiences, that hollers
    And hisses in its own tone, has its own track,
    Stations, destinations, sensations, speed, characteristics,
    Often even different from the past tracks and tricks.
    So, personalities are perpetually in a flux, and stability lack.
That is, one's personality is always changing, different,
    At conflict with one's own past and in every respect!
        For example, a 24-hour old baby, with no memory in store,
Has no 'personality' of any sort; but intent
    On getting food and comfort, if the baby inept
        Starts crying—then who is that?....Not the same any more!

* 25 *

Suppose that a certain individual has an accident
By which he loses memory, and then regains the same
When he has another accident subsequently (blame
This succession of accidents on coincidence or predestiny's
    vent!)
    Such a person is like a new-born baby, with no
    Familiarity with objects, though he wants to learn
    About them, to use them. The same inquisition and urges
        burn
    Within us to recognise things and environments, to know
Them intimately, indicating an innate tendency within us,
    Which is an essence of our true personality and character;
        Even though we need a lot of tools and help from outside.
Let's assume that the amnesia of the patient thus
    Lasted for a year, during which time he labors to gather
        New knowledge and experience, like the new baby who
            cried.

In this manner, he collects knowledge and experience,
Organizing them through association, growing on them.
But as soon as his brain-cells are rejuvenated and the stem
Of his cerebral cortex is able to carry out his mind's sentence,
He'll revive like a person who deeply slumbered
For a while, and is then awakened once again.
The old knowledge and experiences then he'll regain,
No longer needing the memory, carefully stored, numbered,
Accumulated within the short interim time;
He would likely soon forget them. Now how does
The patient view the different personalities —
The different I's versus a single 'I' prime?
What as personality due to sensual perceptions we judge,
Simply turns out to be sort of just a tool on lease.

And yet, there is a more substantial element
Behind all this, which we simply call 'true personality',
Which preserves in these alterations the unique knowlegeable
identity,
And knows: having various experiences—which present
equipment
To use; for peace, physical resources how to strike.
Our white blood-cells voluntarily follow
Their own behavior pattern; our order or will hollow
They await not, nor need our help, and thus are like
As a model of behavior under an absolute
Knowledge or order, bearing an intrinsic pattern.
As soon as viruses enter the body, for instance, and start
Being active, the white cells, sensing the danger acute,
Are prompted into action to fight the virus to earn
Well-being of the body, striving the enemy to outsmart!

The body-temperature rises above the normal to flag
The ongoing battle, and the animal-soul within us becomes
Aware of this struggle, and until the virus succumbs,
The white cells plan their own strategy, without lag,
    To get ready to launch the assault, till this ends
      In the inversion of the enemy's invasion, and the illness is
        uprooted.
      All these types of processes for all types of body-cells led
      To wage all types of wars, continue in all types of trends.
All these activities are, still, in strictly material
    Sphere or domain; there's no will; no spiritual elements,
      Ethical qualities, attributes, are involved here whatsoever.
It is, in fact, certain other types of very real
    Yet transcendental qualities through which the soul paints
      Existence's all pervading, transparent, canvas and picture!

These qualities or qualities of the lighter bodies (called
    "isthmuses")
Are related to the animal-soul or human magnetism,
Which, in turn, are intermediate between the body, wave, and
    soul, in synergism;
They rule over their isthmuses—their existences' special stages.
    Their manifestations and appearances on the nature
    Are according to their predestined dependence on the nature.
    Therefore, events are not the rulers, but rather
    The limited effects of the original premordial picture.
For, how can they be the determinant of something that always
    Existed; clearly it is the 'ever-existent' that immediately
      Determines the boundary of events, and moulds them
        accordingly.
In any event, these continuous interactions and changes
    Of particles and waves cannot give birth to the constant
      reality —
      The soul—and not accepting this would be illogical
      terribly!

When I closely looked at the changes that've taken place
In my body, I see there've been many things I didn't know,
But which I learned. Many of the learnings I used not, and so
I forgot them. There was a time when my mind's face
    Was blank, my soul'd slate clean of emotions' drawings!
    But all these years have gone by, still I am now as then I
    Was. Despite all alterations, any organic change in my
    Identity I do not see....It was 'I' who initiated things;
It was 'I' who decided not to do something; it was 'I'
    Who would compare new information with my stored
        Memory, and accordingly accept or reject a hypothesis;
It was 'I' who can create images in my mind and try
    To preserve them in my memory—Once I get on-board
        My real 'I', my capabilities blossom like the flower's
           genesis!

I've got this facility from the eternal existence:
This 'I' of mine is not confined to any means or form,
So it cannot be known through its attributes or norm —
Specifically attributes that carry ever-changing presence,
    With no stability at all. Therefore, this 'I' who is
    Constant, real and stable in two different times,
    Shall be constant, real and stable at all times. Chimes
    This with Vivekananda's saying, "Each individual in this
World is composed of his true personality—his soul —
    Which lies behind his self. The body
        Is the outer cover and the self is the inner cover
Of the soul; and it's the soul that plays the role
    Of making the body and the self to enact its every
        Wish. The soul is the only true essence that stays over!''

* 32 *

This true essence—the soul—is not material,
And hence, not subject to the laws of causality;
(That is, it's beyond the cycle of cause and effect, pity
And praise, elation and suffering—the worldly emotions trivial
  Associated with the mind or body or any such faction).
  Because of this, the soul is ever - existent,
  Without beginning or end." Not a pretty pendant
  Of a resplendant garland for vain attraction,
But the soul is like the universal pole star!
  Therefore, I've no reason to believe that this
    True essence, which has been constant throughout
My life, I shouldn't consider as existing by far
  Prior to my birth, or after my death. This law thus is
    The declarer of my true essence, the truth's leading scout:

* 33 *

To reiterate, my true essence has been declared, unveiled —
A being that does not change between two arbitrary times,
It's the ever-existent essence. Sing thus certain hymns
On Krishna, who says, "This great universe I've spelled
  Out, created in totality, with my own hands.
  And even though I've done all this, and have lent
  Form to everything, I am not quite apparent
  For everyone. Everything is within me and yet stands
Not touching the absolute essence, not enveloping it!
  Although they are part of me, they're not my true
    Essence. Therefore, ask yourself the question:
What is this mystery—and who is developing it —
  That my soul is able to create everything all through
    But I'm free of everything in this grand procession?"

***

101

Man's natural, unquenchable
Endless expectation,
Desires and longings
Are all layers and linings
Of thick veils of mummification
Over his eyes, making him unable
To see the truth, covering and killing
His own inner vision;
And that's the reason
Why man, like a victim of treason,
Has remained away from his paragon
Happiness, acting like the blind, taking the fake for the real.

***

If, as soon as one had a dream,
It readily in reality bloomed,
And if each desire were to bear
Fruit instantaneously —
The picture of the world would gleam
In happiness; totally doomed
Would be pain, sorrow and care!
— What a change it'd be !

I've seen many people who seem
So infatuated with their own
Day-dreams, Utopia, which gives
Them such pleasure —
That their facial muscles beam
With joy and smiles well sown
On their faces; their mind always lives
In slumber, in buried treasure

Of their own fantasy. They're totally
Out of touch with reality!
I regret to say that, unfortunately,
Dreams have no concrete
Reason; share the truth remotely,
If at all; possess no clarity;
Stand not on pillars stately,
But weak shaky feet!

Immature and infantile illusions
Constantly come to the pages
Of our mind's book, to the screen
Of our mental vision;
And lead to unreal conclusions,
Cover it with colorful haze!
(What blue depression and poison green
For the white soul's unison

They usher, and for the nurture
Of our body of many a color!
As if a miscarriage of imagination
Befalls the pregnancy potent!) —
The poor and the hungry structure
And build bountifully, in galore,
Beautiful castles, for frolic and fun,
Full of dreams, to their heart's content.

(Thus, using the slave labor of the dead
Imagination they bear with care),
Their castle they've provided for
With gold and silver, and stones
Of all colors; and there they're invited
To enjoy fine food, wine rare,
Fancy dresses, women's tresses, or
Whatever their mental hormones

Hanker after and seek gratification
For, instantly, without any hard
Work or preparation or disciplines.
They're no doubt served
Fully, without any bar or reservation,
Even before they discard
Their sword and shield, or host their kins
Or themselves, in their verved

Imaginary, reserved, grand castles,
Standing in their mind-field,
Dazzling tantalizingly in desires'
Domain, in wish-waves afloat!
If these unreal, make-believe annals
Of illogical desires yield
Not; if these wayward wishes' wires
Barbed grab the gate, the moat

Of the brain and the heart too much;
If the vine of the mind gets
Too strong, deep-rooted; if one becomes
Overly drunk; if these opportune
Slaves take over, become rulers as such;
— Then just plentiful regrets
Would survive, for it'd be a most perilous
Trip to heartbreak, calamity, misfortune.

The face of these desires is
Similar to the painted faces
Of prostitutes, who attire themselves
With much deceiving creeds.
But having burnt each bridge
To their souls, they pass their days
In utter pain and unhappiness —
That a self-betrayal breeds....

That penetrate every cell, core,
Trace, depth of their being...
That have changed them truly
Into very dangerous, insensitive
And hard people; yet they allure
Some people as they bring
Out their deceptive looks, duly
The pain and agony to take and give.

Desires are never-ending, infinite!
Whoever, and in whatever condition,
One may be, one is satiated not!
His possessions offer him tranquillity
And peace none, never, nowhere! It
Is readily clear to anyone,
Therefore, (If not, then it ought)
That the building of desires' equity

Is but the land on the sea-shore,
Ladden merely with pebbles, sand —
That can serve to erect no foundation,
To build no pillar, nor to grow
Any grain as whatever water you pour
Disappears into the drinking land,
Leaving it still thirsty; for cultivation
On such a dry land, what'd one sow?

Anyone, then, who says or thinks
That he can quench the thirst
Limitless of such a land, arrest
The denudation and decay
Under the roaring waves, on the brinks
Of hurricanes and storms of the worst
Kind—can only be a fool or jest,
A blundering buffoon at the bay

Of folly profound, searching for
Tranquillity true, fulfillment
Full, in quick urges, indulgence!
He's bound to be swept
Away, scattered, pulverized, or
Dispersed, disintegrated, ill-spent
Aghast, fast becoming past; tense
Anxieties his only creation well-kept!

Whoever is bewitched by desires
Is completely ignorant, without
Any benefit from his soul;
And his thoughts and conscience
Would, whether he wakes up or retires,
Always suffer in the hands, no doubt,
Of many an unknown, undetermined goal
Of desires, the sinking ship of sense!

The day-dreamer creating such illusions
Constantly replays these beautiful
Dreams, thinking he's getting closer
To them each moment. Alas! he
Is like a person gaining intrusions
Only toward a mirage, the bugle
Of vanity ablaze; and exposure
To his self-created grave prematurely!

In the process, he's clearly giving
Up the most sacred treasures
That Existence has given him, just
For whims childish, foolish!
He'd never be achieving
The smallest benefit or heavenly pleasures
That could be long awaiting the trust
And blessing of Existence, its wish!

Existence has given him the bounty;
But he wouldn't reap the smallest
Benefit of his true Self, which
Is the pillar and the greatest source
Of Providence's guidance, Man's lofty
Chance to pass worthily each test,
To overcome every problem, to enrich
Hope against earthly difficulty, despair, remorse!

***

Man has always thought
Of ways to release himself from
Physical and spiritual misfortunes.
Regarding these ways as heavenly boons,
He has always made many a program
To rely on; and in use repeatedly brought.

In the teachings of Buddhism, it's said: "If man should
Know himself, he'd not be bound and chained
To the endless desires of his earthly life, but would look
    upward.
When a person's soul is heeded and spirit stirred,
And he reaches the stage of unrestrained
Revelation, true cognition—for good

His desires disappear automatically.
The strongest chain binding man in this world
Is ignorance—a path opposite to that of knowledge.
He who genuinely chooses the true path of knowledge
Is not misled by gold's glitter, smile of emerald,
Call of pleasure, desire's alley!

He who chooses the dark
Path of ignorance, should definitely end
Up getting lost—wandering without end his only profit!"
For the sage who knows himself, by neither joy's peak nor
    sorrow's pit

Is overwhelmed, consumed, disturbed. Depend
He does not on a need stark

For more or less, good or bad,
Present or future, this or that; fully free
He is, reckoning to his inner voice, his soul's beckoning.
Fichte has said, "Knowledge or cognition is indeed everything
One needs for the basis of the highest degree
Of righteous behavior and

Proper conduct. The person who is
Ignorant or juvenile delinquent in maturity,
Cannot be righteous or doer of good deeds, since he simply can
Not distinguish between right and wrong. In his life-span,
Indeed, every moment, every one, with surety,
Has the freedom of action; so his

Actions can be well-harmonized
With the good, the pure, the pious, and the Godly.
Only if his knowledge and cognition of goodness can open
The door and the way to righteousness—the truth he'll see, only
    then!"
To the utter astonishment of many, oddly
Enough, science has sized

The age of the entire universe!
Researches by scientists on space, fossils, as well
As archeological excavations have managed to unfold the age
Of this planet and of the human history, leaf-by-leaf,
    page-by-page.
Such discoveries and elaborate classifications tell
Us that Man has lived for years

Far less in number than the earth's!
For example, the earth's age is over billion
Years, while Man's, barely one million years. The story of
    Man's evolution

Is like a child's fable in comparison to the epic of the
   progression
Evolutionary of the earth on its endless journey on
The path of astronomical deaths and births!

But the majority of the dwellers
Of the earth—lacking self-knowledge, self-confidence,
Afraid of losing their traditions, inheritance, self-appointed
   centrality
Of gravity, self-identity, illusive crown, universal quality,
Outdated belief in their hollow jurisprudence,
Their dependence on the environment they nurse —

Find it hard to accept, believe
Such ideas, for if they believe in these,
They would feel like little balls on the smooth surface of onyx
Lost as 'nothing' in the middle of the six
Continents and the seven oceans, the heaven at par, star's
   decease,
In the void of death—to ceaselessly grieve!

***

Human beings, during their history's different phases,
Finding themselves completely helpless in the face
Of the forces of nature, watched the rage
Of the clouds, wrath of the thunder, lightnings' race,

   The havoc of the ocean, the sun's terror, lunar games —
   Mysterious charade in the sky; the puzzling play within
   His heart—of fear, torment, guilt and blames,
   Love, affection, war, peace, goodness, sin!

Just about everything around (and within) himself he found
More powerful than he, and he began, quite naturally,
To personify and worship them (as gods), with gestures and
   sound
Of prayers, sacrifices, rituals, gathering centrally.

To Mars, Jupiter, Venus, Uranus, and Neptune,
He offered his worship, in addition to the sun and the moon;
He'd offer sacrifices, chant, sing in sonorous melody, tune
And chorus praising them, seeking their favors and boon,

So they'd protect him from the powerful forces,
And also so he could fulfill his own inner needs,
Aspirations and desires. Hoping secretly his god endorses
His wishes, he would be begging for the seeds

Of happiness and success, freedom from shackles
Of want and fear; he'd pursue much appeasement!
All this he'd do to develop a faith in gods' idols
That he himself created (as symbols that represent

The implicit force or element of nature, unbound).
On especial achievements, instead of believing it was
His own faith and belief and commitment that found
The happy occurrence, the accomplished results, the great
    vistas —

Man would credit everything to his self-created 'gods'.
These illusions he created in his own head —
Without seeing the basic truth, or counting the proper odds —
Would, knowingly or unknowingly, be reinforced, fed

Back to him to his kins, propagating in the society,
And the culture it espouses. This can be seen in some
African tribes (for instance, 'Hottentot', 'Bantu', and
    others) — Thus idle idol-worshippers ignorant people
    become!

The ignorance and lack of knowledge of the early man
Regarding the forces and manifestations of the nature
And the fears they generate truly can
Make an idle idolator of a person of any society, any stature!

During each age under the conditions of the time,
They would worship idols regarded as their protectors,
Giving them the greatest honor and veneration prime,
Some groups following through ritualistic vectors,

Systematically bringing bells and flowers, leaves, incense
And many artifacts to their employ elaborately.
If, in the midst of all this, the worshipper sensed no credence,
If the god of faith didn't fulfil God's faith surrogately,

Did not answer the needs and cravings of each of these
People in accordance with their desires obligingly,
Definitely so many colorful gods and mythological mysteries
Would not have been created, put on pedestals kingly,

Worshipped and surrendered to as the personifications,
    symbols
Of Nature, Existence, Absolute, or the Self, or
The nature's forces, or the inner fears, or mythical dolls —
As the case may be! Nevertheless, often the god for

Whom there should be the highest regard, the most gracious
And kind God, the Gatekeeper of Knowledge and cognizance —
Did not have a place to be worshipped, and thus
Would be noted but little by the people per chance!

Yet, the power and impact, the art and boon of this
God is great, far far greater than the manifestation
Understandable or involved, so much so that the credits amiss
Of his doings were given to other gods of their own creation!

All these existed. However, the deep and effective call
Of the true conscience and the absolute is still
Being heard, without hesitation, each instant, in all
And from behind all these masks people have created (or will).

***

Savagery and civilization both hear
The call of Truth from the speaker;

But the pure ones hear them to hope and become
Its support like pillars, true worshippers—come

What may; it becomes their way of life:
To follow its precepts becomes their daily strife.

In other words, the ones who've aptitude
And capability to follow will be led to extrude

The fate of humanity. It matters not if we
Are devoted to and worship an idol or a tree.

Whether man worships idols in devotion
Or follows spiritual path through intellect, education,

Truth manifests itself equally from behind
The stone idol or the exalted, knowledgeable mind;

And the human civilization is forward led
Either way, as God's Viceregent's whole-hearted

Blessings go to them both, the venues
Of devotion and knowledge and service fuse

Into the same grand highway, leading to self-realization!
— Such people have always been guides to civilization

For mankind, the model of human excellence.
However, that eternal truth, that prime essence —

That Existence has endeavored from the beginning
To impart universality to every human being —

Has been abused much, and used by man's selfishness,
And by society's games, easily making one miss the goal,
    digress.

Xenophon said, "If bulls or lions had hands,
And (assuming the basics of brush their brain understands),

If they could paint with their hands like a human,
Then the painted image (of their god) would be an

Animal—a bull, a lion, and so on—with attributes
Similar to theirs own." In any case, these disputes,

These mistakes, biases and errors that are caused
By internal imbalance, emotional instabilities, aroused

Within one's mind mislead young persons;
Cause mental deviation in the novice who runs

To begin to seek from the most beautiful treasure
He has (himself). This way his standard o'measure

Is shortchanged, however; he's illusioned to seek
Goals which are inconstant, not universal, unique.

Instead of seeking the eternal truth with firm
Dedication, his view is arrested by the short-term

Frames and pictures that become like his gods,
Whose merits he admires and exploits applauds.

Yet these posts he erects can't serve as pillars
Strong for his ascent. Indeed, his own desires, thrillers

Of his mind, and makers of his imagination pert,
Are behind the creation of his gods' images inert,

Which he bears, however, only for the fulfilment of those
Desires and selfish dreams which their effect impose.

So, finally, it's just these desires he does adore;
These desires, then, are his gods—simple desires no more!

—Though he may continue asking the gods for favors
In the disguise of blessings, behind the veil of ignorance, all
   his years!

Spinoza said, "The more a person knows his powers,
The more he can direct himself, even in the darkest hours,

   Onto a selected, solid, strong and sound pathway!"
   And the more one knows of the order, the powerful sway,

And intricate marvellous ways of the Nature, the easier it is
To stay aloof from unnecessary and extraneous things one sees

   All around himself, and the more he can create
   Order in his life, and disorder confiscate!"

***

From the above explanation,
We have to surely agree
That the propagation of illusion
And superstitions essentially

   Occurs by making
   Susceptible and inquisitive
   Minds keep mistaking,
   Go astray, act foolish, misbelieve:

   And in their uncertain
   Quest for their own soul,
   Follow uncertain terrain,
   Play truly a dubious role!

There is none engaged
In the research of the true
Inner being—ignorance be praised!
Though most people do

Keep talking and talking,
A seeker is misled
Under their balking and stalking;
No matter how often it's said

That the goal is within!
If, even at the end of the whole
Story, the realization pristine —
That to reach their goal,

They need someone to guide them, as a foundation sound —
Dawns on them, the search shall continue on this ground!

And the Nature's truth shall be crowned,
And the truth's nature found!

***

Prophet Mohammad
Imam Ali

1. Hazrat Oveys Gharani
2. Hazrat Salman Farsi
3. Hazrat Habib-ibn Rai
4. Hazrat Soltan Ebrahim Adham
5. Hazrat Abu Ali Shaghigh Balkhi
6. Hazrat Sheikh Abu Torab Nakhshabi
7. Hazrat Sheikh Abi Amro Estakhri
8. Hazrat Abu Ja'far Hazza
9. Hazrat Sheikh Kabir Abu Abdollah Mohammad-ibn Khafif Shirazi
10. Hazrat Sheikh Hossein Akkar
11. Hazrat Sheikh Morshed Abu-Esshagh Sharhriar Kazerouni
12. Hazrat Khatib Abolfath Abdolkarim
13. Hazrat Ali-ibn Hassan Basri
14. Hazrat Serajeddin Abolfath Mahmoud-ibn Mahmoudi Sabouni Beyzavi
15. Hazrat Sheikh Abu Abdollah Rouzbehan Baghli Shirazi
16. Hazrat Sheikh Najmeddin Tamat-al-Kobra Khivaghi
17. Hazrat Sheikh Ali Lala Ghaznavi
18. Hazrat Sheikh Ahmad Zaker Jowzeghani
19. Hazrat Noureddin Abdolrahman Esfarayeni
20. Hazrat Sheikh Alaodowleh Semnani
21. Hazrat Mahmoud Mazdeghani
22. Hazrat Amir Seyyed Ali Hamedani
23. Hazrat Sheikh Ahmad Khatlani
24. Hazrat Seyyed Mohammad Abdollah Ghatifi-al-Hassavi Nourbakhsh
25. Hazrat Shah Ghassem Feyzbakhsh
26. Hazrat Hossein Abarghoui Janbakhsh
27. Hazrat Darvish Malek Ali Joveyni
28. Hazrat Darvish Ali Sodeyri
29. Hazrat Darvish Kamal Sodeyri
30. Hazrat Darvish Mohammad Mozahab Karandehi
31. Hazrat Mir Mohammad Moemen Sodeyri Sabzevari
32. Hazrat Mir Mohammad Taghi Shahi Mashhadi
33. Hazrat Mir Mozafar Ali
34. Hazrat Mir Mohammad Ali
35. Hazrat Seyyed Shamseddin Mohammad
36. Hazrat Seyyed Abdolvahab Naini
37. Hazrat Haj Mohammad Hassan Koozeh Kanani
38. Hazrat Agha Abdolghader Jahromi
39. Hazrat Jalaleddin Ali Mir Abolfazl Angha
40. Hazrat Mir Ghotbeddin Mohammad Angha
41. Hazrat Shah Maghsoud Sadegh-ibn-Mohammad Angha
42. Hazrat Salaheddin Ali Nader Shah Angha

Molana-al-Moazam Hazrat Shah Maghsoud Sadegh Angha, Pir Oveyssi has written well over 150 books, treatises, essays and other works on *Erfan* in prose and verse conveyed through different disciplines. These include:

	Written	Published
Psalm of the Gods	1955	1963
Iron	1950	1950
Principles of Faghr & Sufism	1974	1987
The Sufi Miracle	1962-1977*	
Commentary on the Holy Koran - 11 volumes		
Owzan va Mizan (Weights and Balance)	1972	1973
Stages of Cognition in the Holy Koran	1972	1973
Manifestations of Thought	1950	1954
Message from the Soul	1960	1968
The Human Magnetic Body	1970	forthcoming
The Complete Arithmomancy	1967	forthcoming
Chanteh - Realm of the Aref	1940	1943
Life	1970	forthcoming
Microbic Sages	1951	1951
Two Pulse Beats	1973	forthcoming
Remembrance	1965	forthcoming
Al-Salat	1978	1978
Purification & Englightenment of Hearts	1978	1978
The Light of Salvation	1978	1978
The States of Enlightenment	1978	1978
The Hidden Angles of Life	1972	1974
Serr-ol Hajar	1960	1983
The Stages of the Seeker and the Ascent of Nader	1966	1983
The Mantle's Lineage	1945	1945
Through the Gates of the Unseen	1966	1983
The Traditional Medicine of Iran	1976	1978
Love and Fate	1938	1938
The Science of Numbers	1961	forthcoming
The Science of Names	1962	forthcoming
The Science of Coordinates and Squares	1962	forthcoming
The Principles of Oneness (The Epic of Existence)	1966	1968
Ghazaliat	1960	1984
The Star in Literature	1931	1932
Kymya	1961	1972
Golzar-e Omid (The Flowers of Hope)	1963	1964
Nader's Treasure	1940-1979*	
The Rightful Visions	1970	forthcoming
Psalms of Truth	1962	1964
Nirvan	1955	1960
The Heavenly Colors	1960	1984

*being compiled

═══════GLOSSARY OF SELECTED NAMES═══════

The following notes provide very brief biographical sketches of some of the personalities mentioned in the main text. For additional background and detailed information, the reader is referred to the following sources:

Encyclopedia of Islam, Published by E. J. Brill, Leiden (Netherlands), 1913-36 (Second Ed. 1960-); Encyclopedia of Philosophy, Paul Edward (Editor-in-Chief) Macmillan, Inc. and the Free Press, New York (USA), 1972; Biograhpical Encyclopedia of Science and Technology, Isaac Asimov, Doubleday & Co, Inc., Garden City, New York (USA), 1972.

ABOL ABBAS AMOLI: 11th century Persian Sufi. His insight and knowledge of the Holy Koran gave him unbounded facility in the sciences, and his eloquence, spiritual state and wealth of knowledge gained him the admiration of his contemporaries.

ABU SAID ABEL KHEYR: Eleventh century Persian Sufi. He was one of the first to write his religious revelations in verse, in the 'rubai' form. Abu Said became acquainted with Sufism at an early age through his father's interest in Sufism. He completed his formal studies and then pursued his spiritual path, finally meeting Abu Abbas Amoli, through whom he gained his spiritual realization. His vast knowledge, facility in literature and his spirituality drew many devotees and admirers to his circle.

HENRI BERGSON (1959-1941): French philosopher of evolution. He was professor of philosophy at the College de France, was elected to the French Academy and received the Nobel Prize in literature in 1927. Towards the end of his life he was drawn towards religion and mysticism, believing that the mystic's spirit and love were humanity's only hope for a spiritual transformation.

BUDDHA (500 B.C. - 425 B.C.): Indian religious leader, originator of Buddhism. Born as a Prince, the only son to King of 'Kapilvastu' in Nepal near north-eastern India, Sidhartha came to be known as 'Buddha', or the enlightened one, after he renounced the royalty and all worldly attachments to wander in the forests and meditate in search of the transcendental truth and, while in a deep contemplation under a tree, one day attained it. He started preaching to a small group of disciples near Benaras in India not far from the place of his enlightenment, and eventually a large part of Asia including China, Japan, South-East Asia, Burma, Tibet, Sri Lanka, etc. came to accept Buddhism as a way of life.

RENE DESCARTES (1596-1650): French philosopher and mathematician. Sometimes called the father of modern philosophy. He was the originator of the Cartesian system of coordinates and curve-plotting. In his book, "Discourse on Method", published in 1637, he expresses his general skepticism as well as reaffirmation of the strength and value of reason, saying about his own existence "Cognito, ergo sum" - I think, therefore I am.

ALBERT EINSTEIN (1879-1955): German-Swiss-American physicist. Einstein was born at Ulm, Germany and received early education in Munich, Bavaria. He was not a particularly bright student and was scolded by his teacher ("you will never amount to anything, Einstein."), though he was quite interested in mathematics and theoretical physics. After graduation from college, he started working at the Patent Office at Berne, Switzerland in 1901. In 1905, as he earned his Ph.D. degree, he published five papers in the German Yearbook of Physics including one explaining the observed behavior of photoelectric effect on the basis of the quantum theory of light that he propounded for the purpose and that he became a cornerstone of quantum physics. He was awarded the Nobel Prize in Physics for this work in 1921. Of even greater impact and revolutionary nature was his *special* theory of relativity that necessiated a thorough revision of the basic nature of space and time.

GALILEO GALILEI (1564-1642): Italian astronomer and physicist. Galileo was one of the first to herald the Renaissance of science and to stress the importance of quantitative experimental observations. His many contributions included the study of the motion of pendulums, falling bodies, projectiles, and telescopes as well as strength of materials. His discovery that objects of different masses actually fall at equal rate to the earth went against the contemporary belief due to Aristotle, but he experimentally proved the independence of the rate of fall from the object's mass by using inclined planes. His discoveries in mechanics were further developed mathematically by Descartes and Newton.

CHARLES GAUSS (1777-1855): Gauss is regarded as one of the greatest mathematicians of all times. He was educated at the University of Gotingen and made important contributions in theory of curve-fitting, construction of equilateral polygons, theory of numbers, complex variables, and in many other areas of mathematics. He was appointed director of the Gotingen in 1807 and worked on terrestrial magnetism as well as several basic concepts of physics.

SHAMSEDDIN MOHAMMAD HAFEZ: 14th Century Persian Sufi poet. It is said that he was given the name of "Hafez" as a title of respect for someone who has memorized the Holy Koran. Hafez mocked the hypocricy of the clergy in his poems. His poems have been collected under the title of the *Divan*, containing more than 500 poems, most of them being in the form of *ghazals*, traditionally highly structured rhyming couplets. It was Hafez who inspired Goethe to compose his West-ostlicher Divan. His poetry has been translated into many languages; its first English translation was completed in 1891.

HERMAN LUDWIG FERDINAND VON HELMHOLTZ (1821-1894): German physiologist and physicist. Helmholtz studied medicine at Berlin, graduating in 1842 and practicing as a surgeon in the Prussian Army thereafter. He later taught anatomy and physics, invented an opthalmoscope and contributed to the three-color vision (now known as Young-Helmholtz theory), analyzed the scientific principles of the art of music, measured the speed of nerve impulses, and worked on non-Euclidean (Riemannian) geometry. His most important contribution was, however, his formulation of the conservation of energy, stating that energy is converted from one form into another (mechanical or kinetic, heat or thermal, light or electromagnetic, sound, potential, gravitational, chemical, etc.), but never destroyed or created from nothing.

IMMANUEL KANT (1724-1804): German philosopher. Kant studied physics and mathematics, obtaining his doctoral degree in 1755, when he published "General History of Nature and Theory of the Universe". However, he is best known as one of the greatest philosophers and as the author of 'Critique of Pure Reason' published in 1781. In the area of astronomy, he put forward the nebulae hypothesis about the formation of planets, and the suggestion that the Milky Way was a collection of stars and similar other galaxies ("island universes") existed. Under the patronage and protection of Frederick II of Prussia, Kant also contributed freely in the areas of metaphysics.

JOHAN KEPLER (1571- 1630): German astronomer. Although trained to be a minister with graduation in 1591, Kepler developed interest in, and taught, science at the University of Graz in Austria. In 1597, he moved to Prague to work with the famed astronomer Tycho Brahe. In 1609, he published the results of the analyses of Tycho Brahe's accumulated observational data on planetary motion that eventually came to be recognized as the Kepler's laws of planetary motion and which proved to be the stepping stones for the formulation by Newton of the universal theory of gravitation. Kepler also wrote a story, a first science fiction, about a man who travelled to the moon in a dream.

KRISHNA: Hindu deity and mythological figure. Regarded as one of the incarnation or personality of the supreme Godhead ('Vishnu'), Krishna is revered and worshipped in the Hindu tradition throughout India and across the world. Krishna is a central figure of one of the two most popular epics, the 'Mahabharat', written by the sage Vyas. The exact time of composition of these monumental works is not known, but is believed to be earlier than about 5000 B.C.

GOTTFRIED WILHELM LEIBNIZ (1646-1716): German philosopher and mathematician. He was an atomist and was also the first to recognize the importance of the binary system of notation (systems or numbers based only on two states or symbols, 1 and 0)—a system crucial to the operation of modern computers. In 1671 he devised a calculating machine, and in 1684, published important works on calculus. In 1693, he discovered the law of conservation of mechanical energy, subsequently generalized by others for all forms of energy. He was elected a member of the Royal Society of London.

JAMES CLARK MAXWELL (1831-1879): Scottish mathematician and physicist. Maxwell showed sign of genius from his childhood, contributing his first original work to the Royal Society of Edinburgh at the age of fifteen. He graduated from Cambridge and was appointed professor at Aberdeen in 1856. He made major contributions on the structure of the rings of the planet Saturn (1857), the kinetic theory of gases (1860), and the electronmagnetic theory including the nature of light radiation (1864-1873), the last contribution being the well known Maxwell's equations. He died of cancer at the age of forty-eight.

FRANZ ANTON MESMER (1734-1815): German physician. Mesmer, a mystic and astrologer, believed in the existence of cosmic forces affecting everything including human situations. In 1766 he obtained his medical degree at the University of Vienna and turned his attention to finding cure for diseases with the use of magnetic fields, but his success in this venture is doubtful. In fact, he moved in 1778 to Paris; but a commission of experts set up to investigate his methods made an unfavorable report, and he was forced to leave Paris in 1785. He then retired and his technique subsequently came to be recognized by some as curing psychosomatic ailments by suggestion or hypnotism (also called mesmerism in his honor).

SIR ISAAC NEWTON (1642-1727): English scientist and mathematician. He is highly regarded as the discoverer of the theory of universal gravitation, basic laws of motion, and the spectral theory of light. Apart from his superior achievements in many areas of physics, he was also the inventor of calculus, which he applied to formulate laws and solve problems. He was elected to the Royal Society of London in 1672. Like Democritus, Newton believed in a corpuscular nature of light, assuming that light consisted of a stream of particles moving in straight lines, which has certain elements common with the modern quantum theory of light.

PLATO (427 B.C. - 347 B.C.): Greek philosopher. Plato was a devoted follower of Socrates, became his disciple in 409 B.C. and, leaving Athens after Socrate's execution in 399 B.C. he returned to Athens after travelling for 12 years. He founded a school that came to be known as Academy as it was on the grounds belonging to a prominent Greek called Academus. (That first university also subsequently led to the use of the word 'academy' for educational institutes). He remained at the Academy for the rest of his life and died at the age of eighty. Plato's works include a series of dialogues presenting discourses between Socrates and others, chiefly on moral philosophy. He was also very interested in mathematics (The Academy bore the inscription at its doorway, "Let no one ignorant of mathematics enter here"), and applied geometry to the description of the motion of the heavenly bodies.

SOCRATES (470 B.C. - 399 B.C.): Greek philosopher. Socrates is known as an ardent lover of truth and knowledge and for his wit, humor, integrity and courage. He used to lead arguments, to compel his listeners and opponents to admit their own ignorance, even as he displayed modesty and pretended ignorance himself. The Oracle of Delphi proclaimed him the wisest of the Greeks (to which he said: "If I am the wisest it was only because I alone know that I know nothing"). His strong views on ethical code of conduct and his sharp tongue made him be despised by many however, and he was brought to trial in 399 B.C. on charges of atheism and treason. He faced the charges with courage and humor, and finally drank the poison sent for his execution.

HERBERT SPENCER (1820-1903): English sociologist. Spencer had little formal education and remained a lifelong bachelor. He started working in journalism in London around 1846, writing mostly on sociology and psychology. He believed in evolutionary pattern of existence even before publication of the Origin of Species by Darwin, popularizing the term 'evolution' and the phrase 'survival of the fittest'. He advocated practical application of these concepts in the society, justifying brutal competition at the peril of the weak and advancing the doctrine of 'might is right'.

VIVEKANANDA (1863-1902): Indian spiritualist and philosopher. One of the greatest modern exponents and proponents of Indian spirituality, Swami Vivekananda assume his name (Swami = a monk; Vivek = the inner power of discrimination between the real truth against the illusory perception and the untruth; Ananda = divine bliss and inner peace obtained through enlightenment), in place of his given childhood name Narendranath Datta (or, Naren for short), after becoming a disciple of shri Ramkrishna, a present-day mystic-

125

spiritualist in the tradition of the ancient sages, whose inspiration led him to become a monk and later to come to the United States to attend the Parliament of Religions (Chicago, 11-27 September, 1893).

XENOPHANES (570 B.C. - 480 B.C. approx.): Greek philosopher. Xenophanes was contemporary to the mathematician Pythagoras well-known for Pythagoras theorem on right angle triangles (the square of the hypotenuse equals the sum of the squares of the other two sides). He postulated the emergence of the ground from the receding waters of the seas based on the observation that sometimes sea-shells are found on mountain-heights. This is recognized as a valid assumption by modern geologists. Unlike many of his contemporaries, Xenophanes did not believe in transmigration of the soul or in the multitude of Greek gods.